every morning

1/100th Second Mikrograph

1916

1966

1/10,000th Second
Indy 500

2004

150 YEARS PIONEERING SWISS WATCHMAKING FOR 150 YEARS

SWISS AVANT-GARDE SINCE 1860

ASSOULINE

Introduction. This is the story of speed, of the hunt for speed, of catching time, of mastering time. This is the story of TAG Heuer, the legendary Swiss master of ultimate precision. Every story starts with a man and a passion. Edouard Heuer had the vision of time. The man became a team, a passionate team. And the road became a speedway of legendary competitions linking today's most powerful men and women, the heroes of their eras, in a "race against time." To catch time was also the design. Humanity's progress is fueled by this aim, and our identity has always been influenced by the biggest names in architecture, art, and avant-garde design of each generation.

But let's return to the story: a suite of challenges, conquests, and innovations that started in 1860, 150 years ago, when Edouard Heuer began his competition with time. In 1882, a little more than a decade before the first modern Olympics, he created his first chronograph, a timepiece that has maintained its precision and speed ever since. In 1887 he patented the Oscillating Pinion, a major component still in use today in the best Swiss mechanical chronographs. By the early twentieth century, TAG Heuer had moved the chronograph from the pocket onto the wrist. In 1916, mere fifths and tenths of a second were already crude interstices, but TAG Heuer created a new balance wheel oscillating at a stunning speed of 360,000 vibrations per hour. Here was a mechanical stopwatch capable of calibrating elapsed time to the nearest hundredth of a second. Modern men and women could now pit themselves on the track, on horseback, on skis, in the air, or even challenge the records of medical and industrial progress. TAG Heuer chronographs would travel into a new dimension of timekeeping with the advent of electronic timing sixty years later. In 1966, Jack Heuer, great-grandson of the founder, pushed timekeeping to new limits with the miniaturized electronic Microtimer, accurate to one-thousandth of a second, a new milestone in mastering time. Ironically, though, the electronic age has seen the renaissance of mechanical timekeeping, with the first-ever automatic chronograph with microrotor, launched in 1969 in the iconic Monaco, TAG Heuer Carrera, and Autavia lines. Since then TAG Heuer has developed both mechanical and electronic timekeeping to new levels of accuracy and reliability. Today sports champions and international personalities alike identify with TAG Heuer's passionate story: a zeal for challenge and ceaseless innovation embodied by the company motto: "Swiss Avant-Garde since 1860."

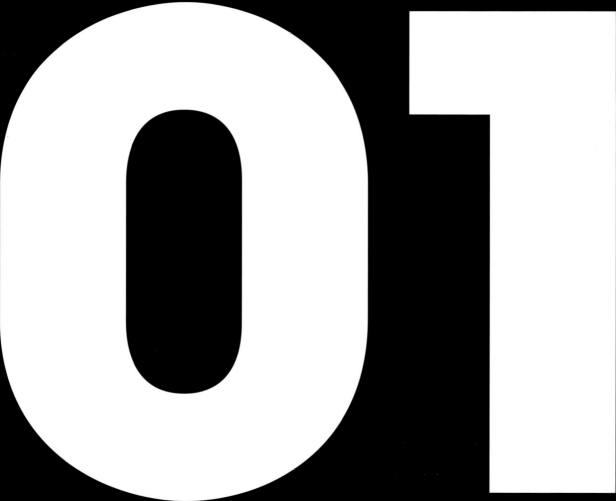

History. The quest for speed is one of humanity's perpetual goals. And yet without time, speed is nothing. Time is the cruelest master of all; unforgiving, untiring, irreversible, it is our sternest judge. It is the quest to master time that has shaped and obsessed TAG Heuer for the past 150 years.

World history often turns on the will of a single man, and the same is true for the history of watchmaking. In the mid-nineteenth century, a Swiss shoemaker's son named Edouard Heuer made the decision to turn over his life to the conquest and calibration of the passing hours, minutes, seconds, and fractions of seconds, marking their passage with the tiny incremental movements of the blued steel hand of a chronograph against the crisp white enamel dial of the pocket watch. From childhood Edouard was dazzled by the dream of conquering time and imprisoning it in ever-more precise and advanced mechanical timepieces. From his apprenticeship at the age of fourteen until his untimely death at the age of just fifty-two, he was obsessed with innovation as he pursued ever-greater accuracy. In 1882, as sports became more competitive, he introduced his first chronograph, then upgraded it in 1887 with the famous Oscillating Pinion component, a milestone in high-end watchmaking history. It is a trite truism to talk of the DNA of a brand, but Edouard Heuer composed the opening chapter of a story that is still unfolding. TAG Heuer today continues the mission of its founder, questing for the more exact and forensic measurement of ever-smaller parcels of time, quantities almost too small to be grasped by thought. These tiny increments are paradoxically the largest component of the brand's genetic heritage.

While much in the world may have changed, the essential, elemental nature of humanity's struggle to master time and to move faster through it remains much as it was when Edouard Heuer embarked on his journey. And, 150 years on, as remarkable men and women continue to compete against one another and that ultimate adversary, time itself, TAG Heuer remains at their side and on their wrists.

1860

This page: Edouard Heuer's hunting watch, 1860. Opposite: The Monaco V4.

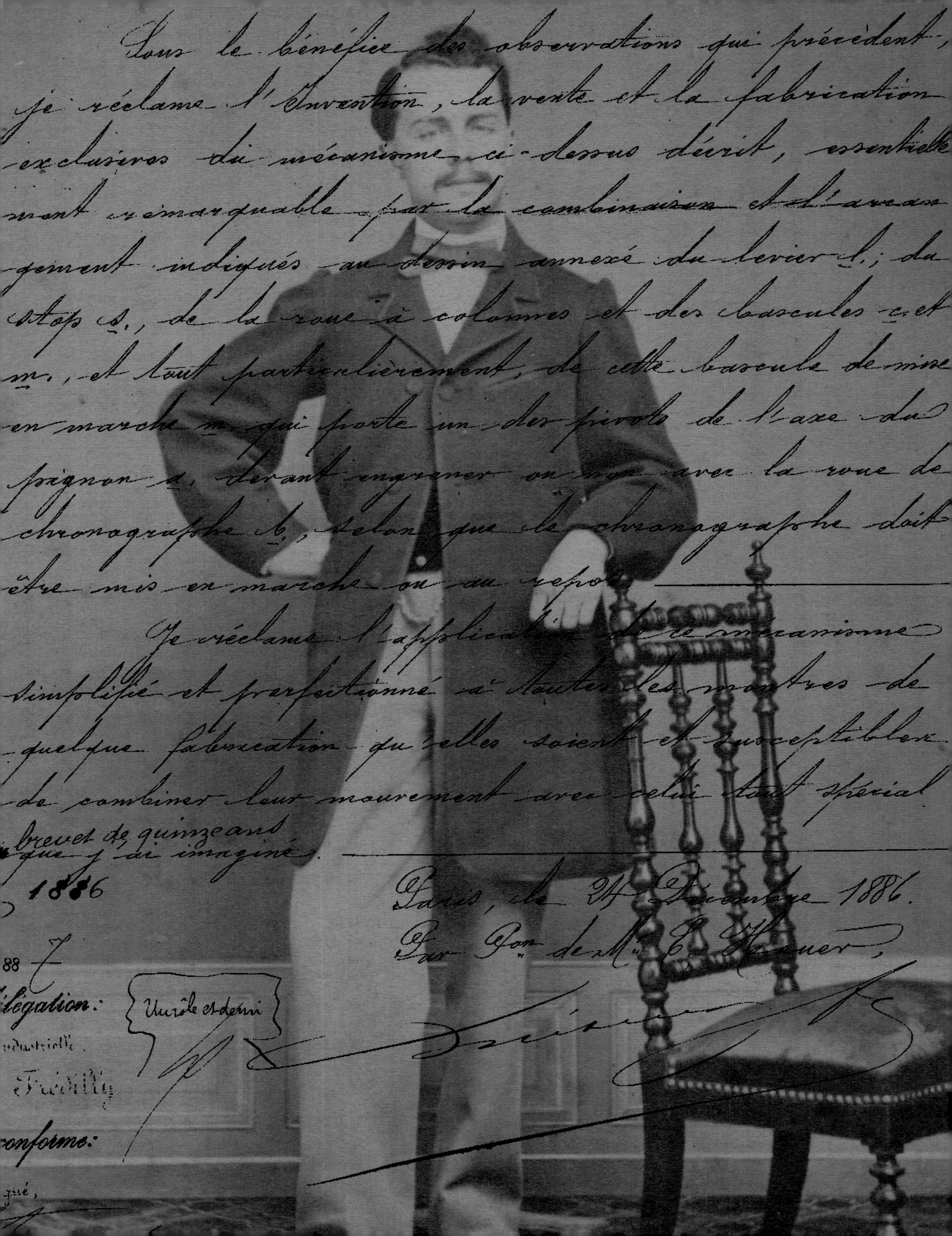

Sous le bénéfice des observations qui précèdent, je réclame l'invention, la vente et la fabrication exclusives du mécanisme ci-dessus décrit, essentiellement remarquable par la combinaison et l'arrangement indiqués au dessin annexé du levier l, du stop s, de la roue à colonnes et des bascules c et m, et tout particulièrement, de cette bascule de mise en marche m qui porte un des pivots de l'axe du pignon a, devant engrener ou non avec la roue de chronographe b, selon que le chronographe doit être mis en marche ou au repos.

Je réclame l'application de ce mécanisme simplifié et perfectionné à toutes les montres de quelque fabrication qu'elles soient et susceptibles de combiner leur mouvement avec celui tout spécial que j'ai imaginé.

brevet de quinze ans

1886

Paris, le 24 Décembre 1886.
Par Pon de M. E. Heuer,

> "My crown-winding mechanism can be used on all kinds of watches. Simplicity is its most distinguishing characteristic… Thanks to the parts of which it is composed, it is independent from the movement and it is no longer necessary to take apart the moving parts to repair it…"

Edouard Heuer

1860 Edouard Heuer (1840–1892) founds the Heuer company in Saint-Imier, Switzerland.

1. Charles-Edouard Heuer (1896–1974), aged 11 and wearing a cadet's suit, 1907. **2.** Maria-Hortense-Ida Blösch (1874–1939) in 1893, shortly before her marriage to Charles-Auguste Heuer in 1895. She was the daughter of a major steel-wire manufacturer whose wedding gift to his new son-in-law was a large share in the Trévileries Réunies Company of Bienne. **3.** Louise-Honorine Heuer (1861–1887), Edouard Heuer's daughter, 1880. **4.** Edouard Heuer (1840–1892), 1890. **5.** Jules-Edouard Heuer (1864–1911), Edouard's son, ca. 1910. **6.** Charles-Auguste Heuer (1871–1923), Edouard Heuer's second son, around 1890. **7.** Heuer participated in the first Basel Watch Fair in April 1934. From left to right: Emile Juillard,

Ferdinand Cuanillon, Frédéric Cuanillon, Louis Cuanillon, Charles-Edouard and Hubert Heuer, Charles-Auguste's sons. **8.** Heuer workshop and house in Bienne, rue des Vergers, 1889. This building would be Heuer's house and workshop for three generations. **9.** Hubert, a client, Charles-Edouard, and his son Jack Heuer in 1965. **10.** Hubert Heuer (1901–1978) around 1970. **11.** Hubert Heuer and his sister Germaine playing in front of Heuer's house-workshop, ca.1906–1907. **12.** The Heuer workshop and house in Brügg, 1860. **13.** Charles-Edouard Heuer around 1960. **14.** Jack Heuer (1932–), aged 4 and wearing short trousers in 1936 at Saignelégier. **15.** Jack Heuer, 1954.

> **"It is sometimes useful to see how things happen elsewhere... We learn a lot of things that we would never even have thought of at home."**

Jules and Charles Heuer
in a letter to their mother from London, May 30, 1899

1922 This family tree, based on Charles-Auguste Heuer's genealogical research, presents 10 generations of Heuers, from the 16th century to the 20th.

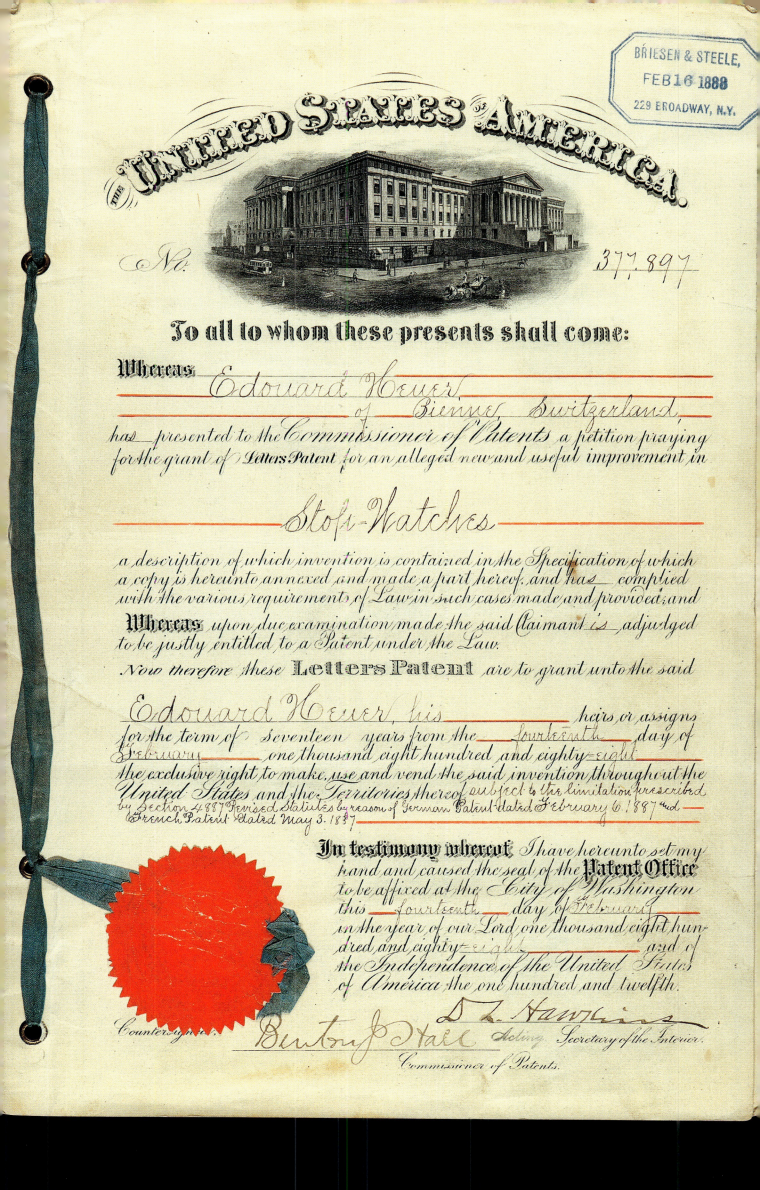

1911 Heuer patents the Time of Trip, the first dashboard chronograph for aircraft and automobiles. Two large blue hands at the center of the dial indicate the hours and minutes. The pair of small hands located at 12 o'clock give the duration of a trip less than twelve hours long. The single push button is used to start, stop, and reset the chronograph function to zero. The small window at 3 o'clock indicates whether this function is working.

1916 Heuer invents the Microsplit, the world's first 1/100th-of-a-second stopwatch with a split-second hand.

1920 This page: gold wrist chronograph with enameled dial; large, luminous digits; and a push button at 2 o'clock that starts, stops, and resets the chronograph function to zero. Opposite: Hubert Heuer in 1921.

1928

As a pioneer, Edouard Heuer began with the basic premise that if we can measure it, we know we can better it.

Heuer timekeeping stand during a 1928 ski competition.

1950 Heuer unveils its patented Mareograph, the first chronograph with a tide indicator and a five-minute countdown function for sailing competitions.

1958 The legendary Rally-Master is a combination of a Master-Time and a Monte-Carlo. In addition to an eight-day power reserve, the Master-Time watch has a mechanism that synchronizes with the central control timer. The Monte-Carlo stopwatch indicates elapsed time with a 60-minute counter and a 12-hour numerical jumping disc that greatly improved legibility.

1959 Jack Heuer and his father, Charles-Edouard, in the Heuer factory in Bienne.

1959 Ken Wyley, a Heuer watchmaker in the American subsidiary based in New York, at 441 Lexington Avenue.

1960 Heuer's Basel Watch Fair booth celebrates the company's 100th anniversary (1860–1960).

1962 This page: On February 20, astronaut John Glenn makes the first American manned Earth-orbital mission, circling the planet 3 times in 5 hours. He is wearing a Heuer stopwatch, reference 2915A, on his wrist. Heuer becomes the first Swiss company to go into space. Opposite: The same year, the company introduces the Autavia wrist chronograph, after producing the Autavia dashboard timer from 1933 to 1958.

1968 After the launch of the Film-Master in 1963, designed to meet the special requirements of Hollywood directors, the company launches the TV Film-Master, which allows directors to time the length of their 16-millimeter and 35-mi limeter films.

1969 This page: Heuer launches the Chronomatic Calibre 11, the world's first automatic chronograph movement with a microrotor. Three series are outfitted with this movement: the Autavia, the elegant TAG Heuer Carrera, and the new Monaco series. Opposite: In the racing film *Le Mans* (released in 1971), actor Steve McQueen wore the Heuer logo on his overalls and the legendary Monaco chronograph on his wrist.

1971 As Official Timekeeper for Formula One, TAG Heuer makes clear that beyond every finish line is another starting line.

The Heuer company develops the Le Mans Centigraph during its appointment as Official Timekeeper for the Scuderia Ferrari in 1971. This timing instrument, composed of keyboards and a printer, measures to 1/1,000th of a second.

1975 Jack Heuer debuts the Chronosplit, the world's first quartz wrist chronograph with a double digital display (LED and LCD) that measures to 1/10th of a second. Enzo Ferrari orders a limited edition of 15 pieces with the Ferrari logo.

1. The "Don't crack under pressure" advertising campaign (BDDP) featuring Ayrton Senna, TAG Heuer Ambassador from 1988 to 1994. 2. The "What are you made of?" 2009 campaign (CLM/BBDO) featuring Maria Sharapova, TAG Heuer Ambassador since 2005. Photo by Tom Munro for TAG Heuer. 3. Advertisement, 1930. 4. The "Inner Strength" campaign (BBH) featuring Boris Becker, TAG Heuer Ambassador from July 1997 to June 2000. Photo by Anton Corbijn. 5. "Le chronographe par excellence" campaign, 1945. 6. The "Success: it's a mind game" campaign (BDDP). Photo by Russell & Connie Guzman, 1995. 7. "Le chronographe par excellence" campaign, 1944.

8. "Le chronographe par excellence" campaign, 1943. 9. The "Beyond measure" campaign (TBWA) featuring Steve McQueen, 2000. 10. The "What are you made of?" campaign (TBWA) featuring golf great Tiger Woods, TAG Heuer Ambassador since 2003. Photo by Guido Mocafico. 11. The "What are you made of?" 2009 campaign (CLM/BBDO) featuring Leonardo DiCaprio, TAG Heuer Ambassador since December 2008. Photo by Tom Munro for TAG Heuer. 12. The "Pioneering Swiss Watchmaking for 150 Years" campaign (CLM/BBDO), 2010. Photo by Tom Munro for TAG Heuer. 13. "Perfect gift for sportsmen" advertisement, 1959. 14. Advertisement, 1955.

2003 Speed is merely a m[a]
Being fast is all about being

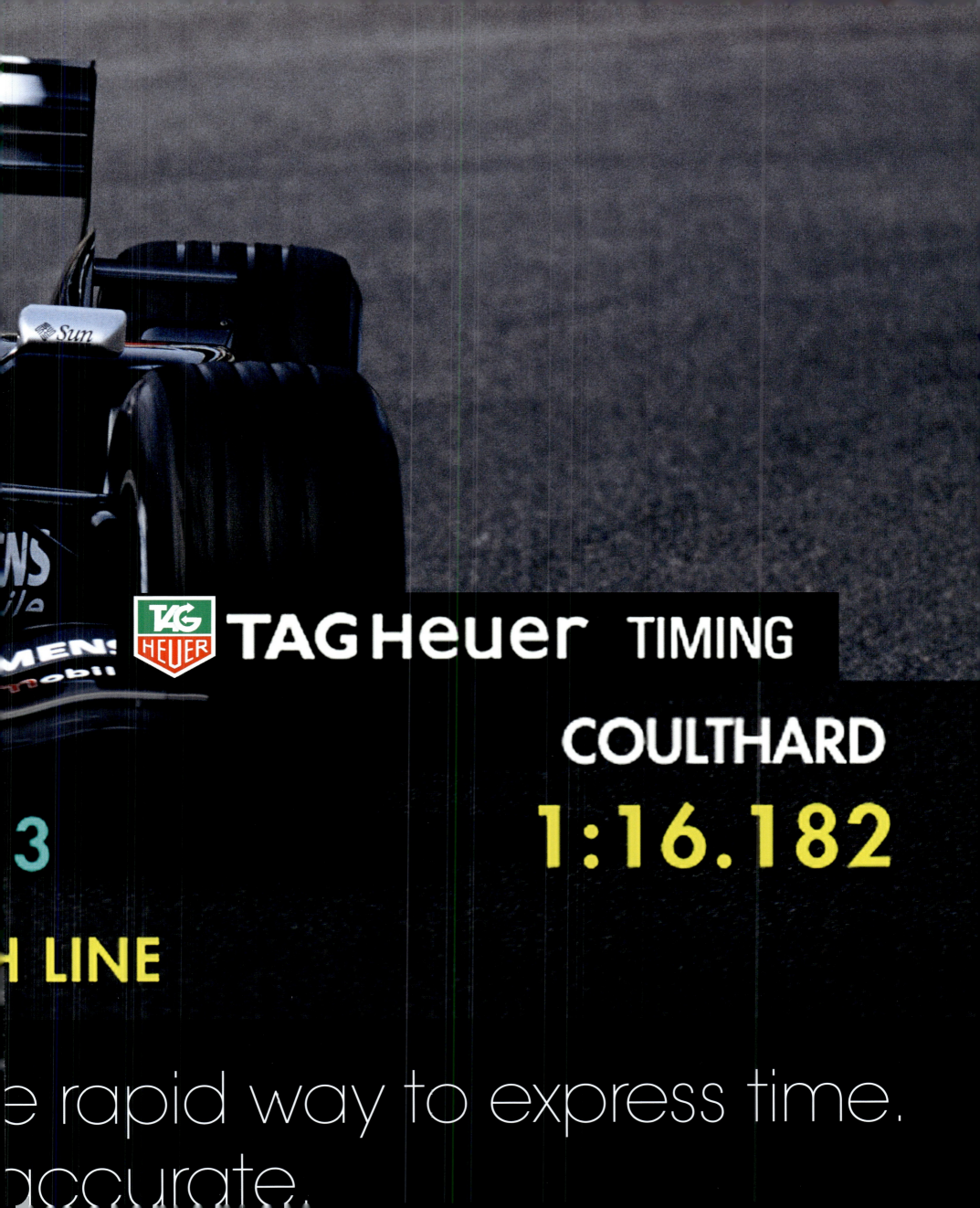

2003 The TAG Heuer Carrera Calibre 7 Twin-Time, an automatic watch with two time zones.

1969

2008 The TAG Heuer 360 museum, La Chaux-de-Fonds, Switzerland.

02

Mastering time. TAG Heuer has developed both mechanical and electronic timekeeping to new levels of accuracy and reliability, and twenty-first century technology has enabled TAG Heuer to take humanity's understanding of time on a journey to the threshold of one of the most elusive and alluring figures in international sports timing: the ineffable ten-thousandth of a second.

TAG Heuer's enviable legacy in the field of sports timing is unique. It was Jack Heuer, great-grandson of Edouard, who made the decisive move into motor racing. Like the generations before, Jack was fascinated by sports timing and was quick to see the huge potential of linking the worlds of motor sport and precision timing.

In America, the company supplied the timing equipment for Sebring. Jack Heuer started to hang out with drivers, coming to understand their distinctive mentality and appreciate the significance and often-mythical status of the great motor races. In 1964 a great watch was born, the TAG Heuer Carrera, which would later be joined by the Monaco and the Silverstone.

The brand's association with Ferrari came about in 1971 with the creation of the Le Mans Centigraph, a timer and printer to identify the car, the number of laps, the lap time, and the total time. The relationship deepened during that decade, when every Ferrari driver wore the company logo on his overalls and made a pilgrimage to the factory to pick up a gold chronograph engraved with his name and blood type. All the Ferrari cars, from the 24 Heures du Mans to Formula One, featured the famous red shield on their fronts. Over the decades, the roll call of drivers associated with the brand has included many of the true greats: Clay Regazzoni, Jo Siffert, Niki Lauda, Ayrton Senna, 2007 world champion Kimi Raïkkönen, and 2008 world champion Lewis Hamilton, and TAG Heuer is proud to have been a part of the McLaren team since 1985. From 1992 until 2003, TAG Heuer was also the Official Timekeeper for Formula One, and since then it has been affiliated with the Indianapolis 500.

Wheels, discs, driving belts, ultimate technical material, high-tech tubular design, extreme shock-protected components, and composite filters—the inspiration from motor racing seems endless. TAG Heuer even adapted the idea of the concept car to watchmaking, with a stunning series of concept watches and chronographs honored at the Grand Prix d'Horlogerie de Genève. Inspired by Le Mans endurance race cars and epitomized by the recent MONACO *Twenty Four* Concept Chronograph, this combination of manual craftsmanship with technology based on motor-racing advancements and on a century and a half of watchmaking expertise is what TAG Heuer is made of.

In a wider sense, the coordination of a motor-racing team finds its reflection in the intricate jigsaw puzzle of skills and talents that come together to create a timepiece: designers, engineers, and watchmakers, all performing several hundred operations in harmony to create a living machine from hundreds of tiny high-tech parts.

But TAG Heuer cannot be reduced to a racing inspiration. The company has been a fixture in diving and sailing since it introduced the first water-resistant chronograph case in 1895. The Mareograph, featuring a tide indicator, came in 1950, and is today the global standard for stylish and upscale diving-inspired timepieces. TAG Heuer also broke ground in the filmmaking world when it introduced the Film-Master in 1963, which allowed directors to more easily sequence their movies. The brand became a Hollywood and Bollywood favorite, and TAG Heuer timepieces regularly appeared on the wrists of artists and actors, in their movies as well as in their daily lives.

And from TAG Heuer laboratories and workshops, design studios, and test centers high in the mountains of Switzerland, in La Chaux-de-Fonds and Cornol, a torrent of innovation continues to flow. Hours of meticulous craftsmanship and years of research and design development have given birth to the Microtimer, the first wrist chronograph accurate to one-thousandth of a second; the TAG Heuer Carrera Calibre 360 Concept Chronograph, the first mechanical wrist chronograph to measure and display one-hundredth of a second; while the Link Calibre S is the first electromechanical chronograph accurate to one-hundredth of a second and is fitted with a retrograde perpetual calendar.

In 2007 TAG Heuer presented the TAG Heuer Grand CARRERA chronograph, an entirely mechanical series. C.O.S.C.–certified and equipped with the revolutionary Calibre RS (Rotating System), it is the first to display tenths of a second not with traditional hands, but with a system of turning discs.

TAG Heuer's work is never finished, and the brand is developing an in-house mechanical chronograph column-wheel movement with automatic rewind, the new Calibre 1887. Designed to meet the highest expectations of timekeeping and precision, it will be launched in 2010, just in time for the 150th anniversary of TAG Heuer. The Calibre 1887 completes a trilogy of exceptional movements that TAG Heuer will present in 2010, along with the Monaco V4, featuring the world's first movement to use notched driving belts and linear mass mounted on ball bearings, and the new Calibre Mikrograph 1/100th, the improvement of the Calibre 360 from 2005, both in limited editions.

Opposite: The TAG Heuer Calibre 1887, an automatic chronograph movement made entirely in-house and scheduled for launch in 2010 for the company's 150th anniversary. From top to bottom: the main plate, the movement, and the gear train bridge.
Following pages: Escape wheels and pictures taken by a camera filming at 5,000 frames per second in the TAG Heuer test laboratory.

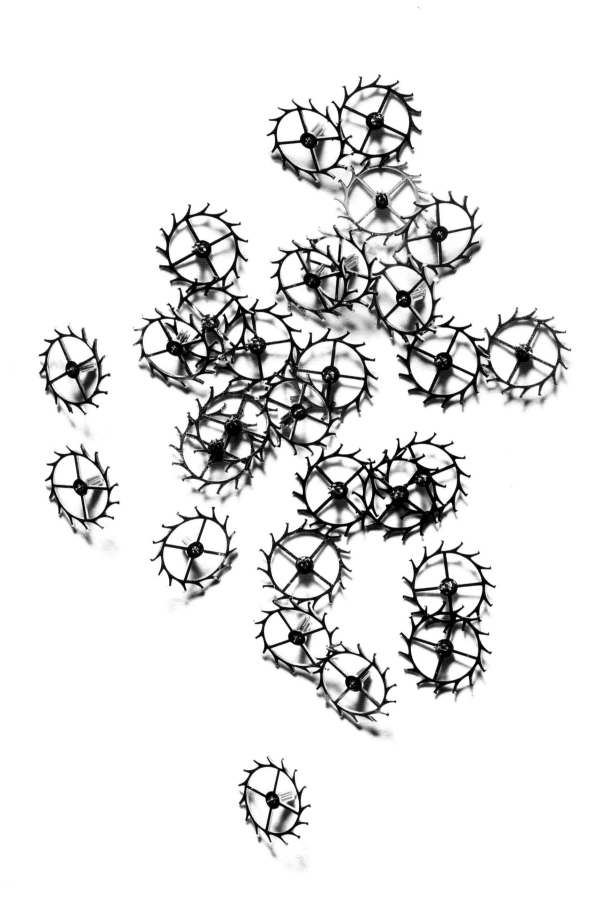

This page: The Diamond Fiction concept watch, the first watch ever to display time through illuminated diamonds, 2005.
Opposite: Dial manufacturing at Artecad, 2007.

This page: The parts of the TAG Heuer Calibre 360 Concept Chronograph, the first automatic chronograph to measure and display time to 1/100th of a second, 2005.
Opposite: The Calibre Mikrograph 1/100th, the improvement of the Calibre 360, will launch in 2010.

From hundreds of parts

a synchronized whole...

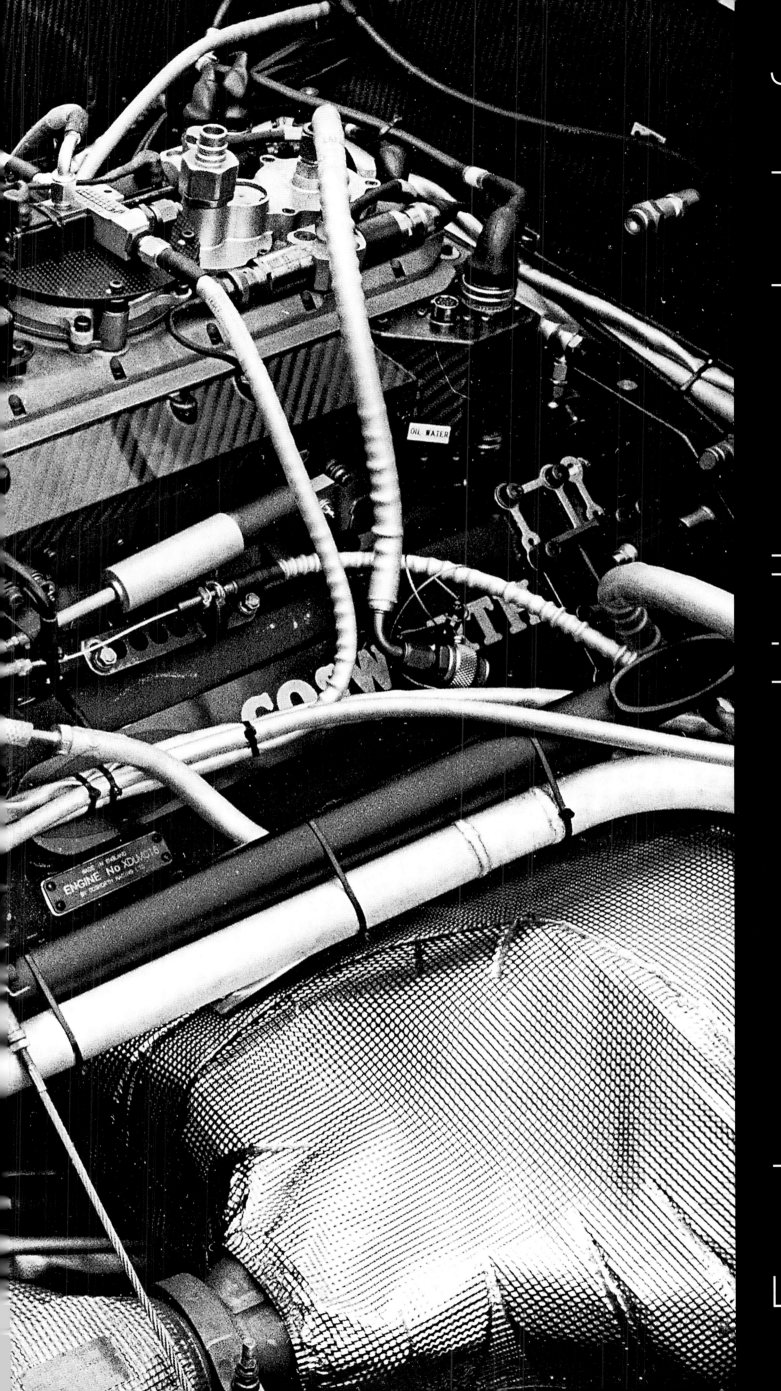

Each component is the product of a different technology, and yet the sum is greater than its parts.

This page: In 2003, TAG Heuer presented the Monaco *Sixty Nine*, the first reversible watch with two different displays and movements assembled in one case. One side has the analog Monaco dial with a mechanical movement, the other side has the digital Microtimer measuring to 1/1,000th of a second.
Opposite: Watchmakers at work in the Heuer workshop in Bienne, 1963.

This page: Final inspection of a TAG Heuer Carrera Calibre 16 Chronograph, TAG Heuer workshop.
Opposite: Jacky Ickx in his Formula One car, German Grand Prix, 1972.
Following pages: Valjoux movement Calibre 9, ca. 1960s; conditioning of the TAG Heuer Grand CARRERA dials.

> "Creativity and quality, our key values, our priorities."

Bernard Arnault
Chairman & Executive Officer of LVMH

Previous pages: Lewis Hamilton comes in for a pit stop during the Malaysian Formula One Grand Prix at the Sepang circuit on March 23, 2008, in Kuala Lumpur. Opposite: Tough enough to withstand the demands of professional competition, TAG Heuer sports watches undergo some 60 different quality controls before release, including tests for pressure and water resistance.

Hand-setting of a stopwatch in the Heuer workshop in Bienne, 1990.
Following pages: Live timing data screen, 2003.

The TAG Heuer team trains daily to make mankind a time machine worthy of the human machine.

This page: Muddled movements/vibration tests. Opposite: Link DDDB chronograph, 2008.
Following pages: Traction and torsion test for bracelets.

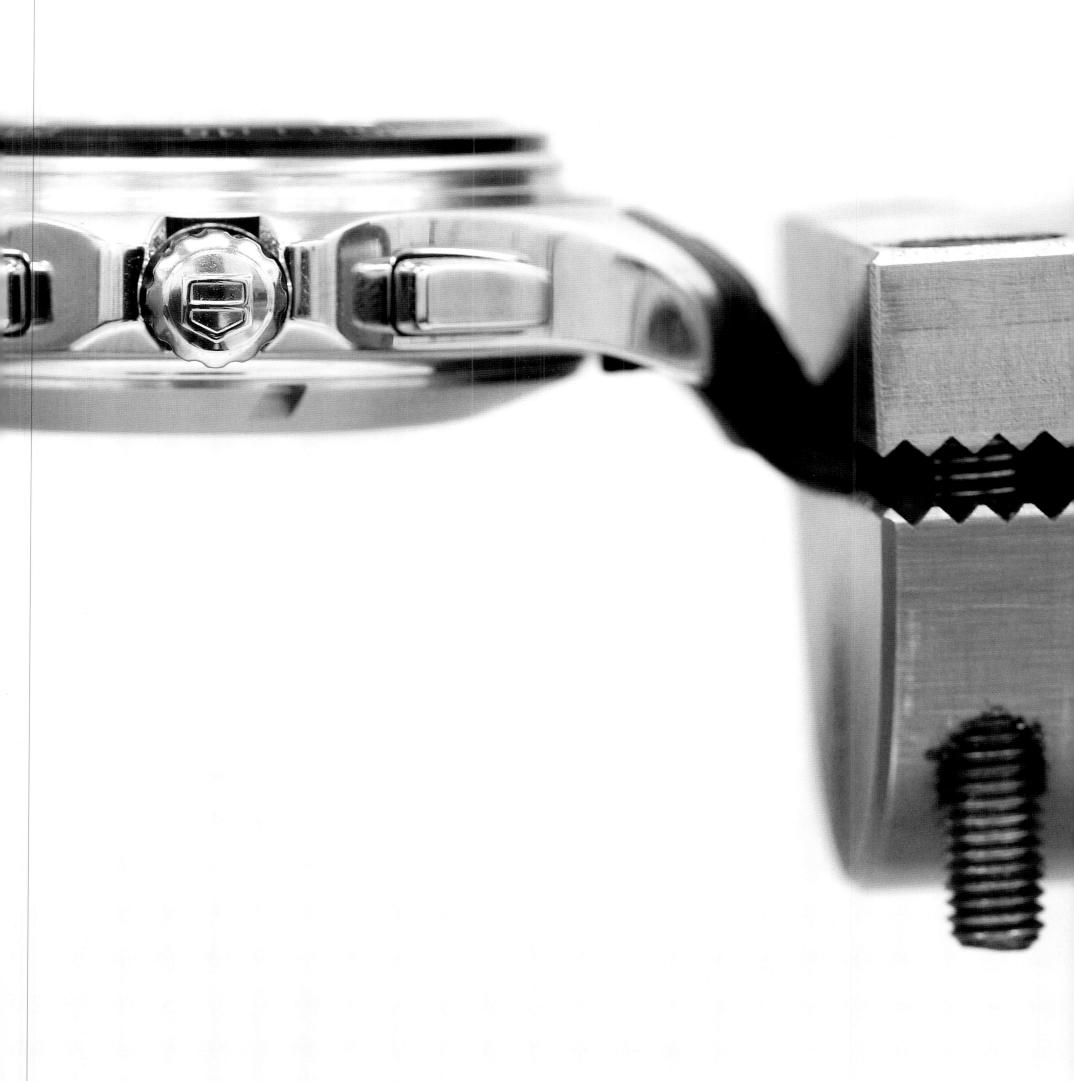

This page: Calendar bridge from the Calibre 12.
Opposite: The dials of the TAG Heuer Grand CARRERA Calibre 17RS 2 automatic chronograph.

This page: Alain Prost in the McLaren car, Monaco Grand Prix, May 11, 1986.
Opposite: The Microsplit 370 wrist stopwatch, designed by Richard Sapper in 1976, with liquid crystal display that allows for split timing.

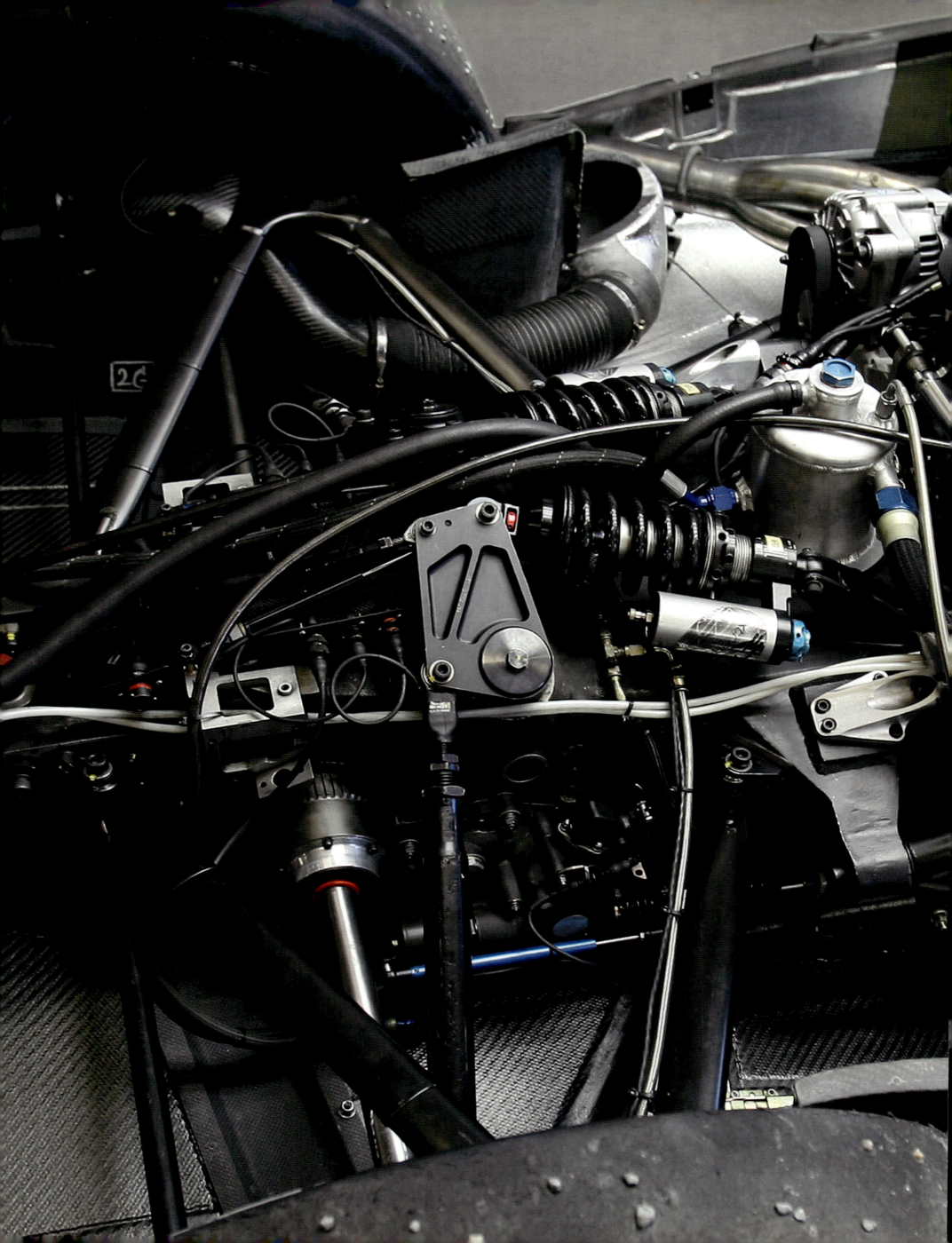

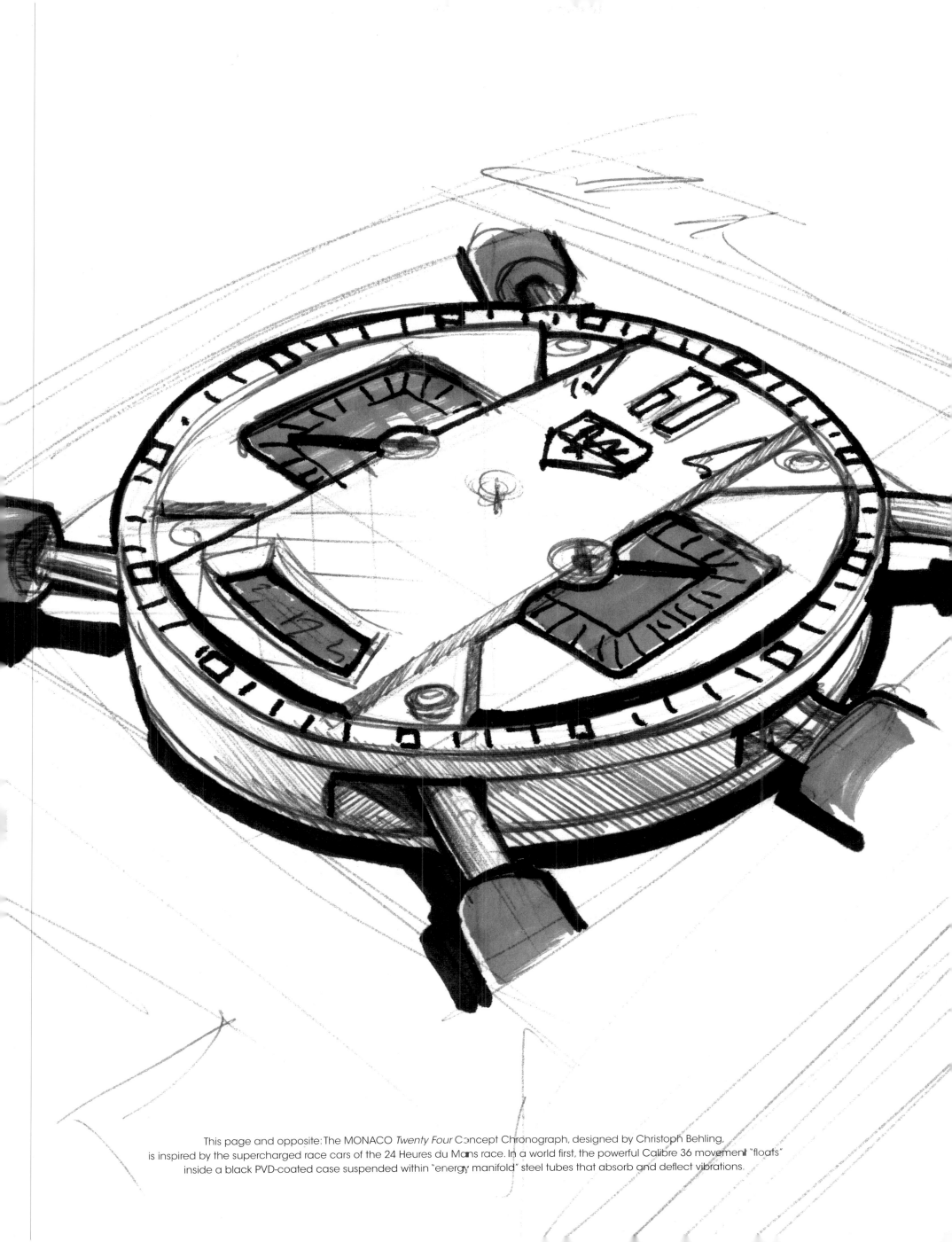

This page and opposite: The MONACO *Twenty Four* Concept Chronograph, designed by Christoph Behling, is inspired by the supercharged race cars of the 24 Heures du Mans race. In a world first, the powerful Calibre 36 movement "floats" inside a black PVD-coated case suspended within "energy manifold" steel tubes that absorb and deflect vibrations.

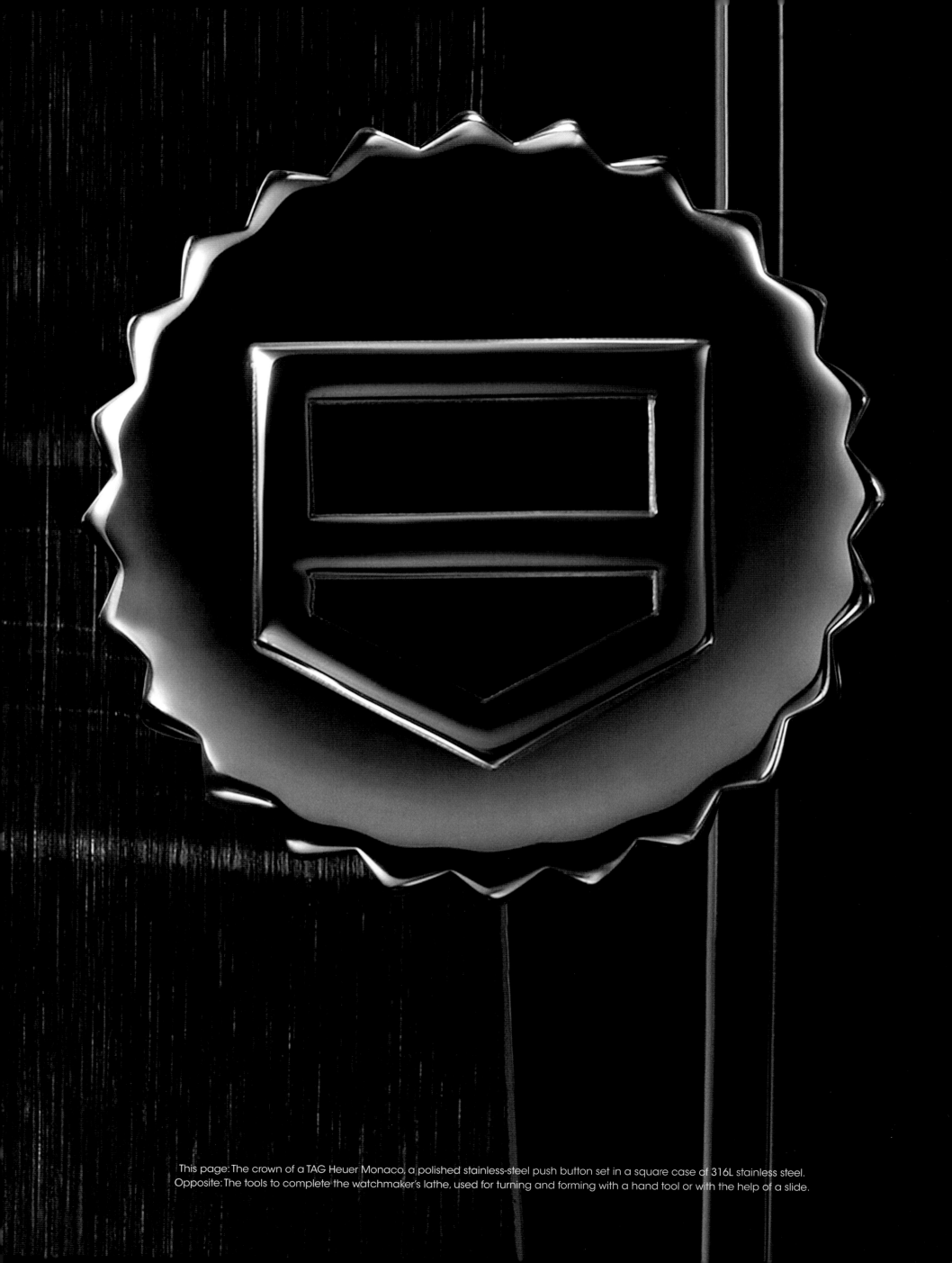

This page: The crown of a TAG Heuer Monaco, a polished stainless-steel push button set in a square case of 316L stainless steel.
Opposite: The tools to complete the watchmaker's lathe, used for turning and forming with a hand tool or with the help of a slide.

03

Design. Adapted for environmental extremes, multifunctional, and self-repairing, the human body is by far the most remarkable of all the machines ever designed. At TAG Heuer, design, both internal and external, has harnessed every technological advance to give mankind a time machine worthy of the human machine. Bold, striking, innovative above all—TAG Heuer has been defined by an understanding that the process of design is not an abstract science, but one of practical application rooted in historical context.

The timepieces of each age have their architecture: the large, fingertip-friendly winding crowns and pusher of those early wrist-worn chronographs; the groundbreaking Calibre 11 automatic chronograph movement of 1969, which signaled its presence with a big square case, winding crown at 9 o'clock, and a daring blue dial when all watches were boringly round, slim, and white; or the stunning belt-driven movement of the Monaco V4, its internal beauty made visible through a faceted crystal case back.

But a wristwatch is not an object created in isolation, and it has a strong architectural influence. As a piece of design, it holds a mirror up to art and architecture on a grander scale. The Monaco, for example, is as bold and uncompromising as Le Corbusier's Villa Savoye, a machine designed for living. Indeed, there is an unmistakable and unapologetic vigor about such designs from the 1970s as the Chronosplit Manhattan GMT, with its polyhedral case, which echoes the iconic profile of New York City's dynamic skyline. From the same period, there's also the Microsplit, which has the perfect simplicity of an Oscar Niemeyer arch in cast concrete. It's a masterpiece in miniature, with all superfluous detail stripped away. And TAG Heuer has recently applied its understanding of innovative, function-driven form to eyewear and communications technology. At TAG Heuer, design is not finite; it is a process that constantly evolves. While it is possible to recognize the antecedence of the modern wrist-worn chronograph in those early timepieces, design, like time, is never allowed to stand still. Thus the straps and buckles that once seemed so avant-garde compared with the watch chains of an earlier generation of timekeepers now seem antique when compared with the fluid ergonomics of the stepped and rounded ligaments of the Link bracelets. These in turn give way to the innovative alliance of a minutely adjustable rubber strap, daring combination case, and folding buckle on the Professional Golf Watch, designed with Tiger Woods to sit close to the human wrist and feel like an extension of the wearer's own arm. As the natural progression of the original TAG Heuer Carrera, the TAG Heuer Grand CARRERA Calibre 36 RS Caliper Concept Chronograph is a powerful fusion of sleek design and visionary technology, a revolutionary new way of telling time.

This is how classics are born at TAG Heuer: out of ceaseless evolution and improvement at the point where technical virtuosity, imagination, and ingenuity meet.

Avant-garde technology. TAG Heuer MERIDIIST, the first-ever Swiss-engineered luxury communication instrument, launched in 2008.

Purity of shape and form. This page: The S/el bracelet, with its signature S-shaped links, is a worldwide reference for flexibility, wearer comfort, timeless aesthetics, and peerless ergonomics. It's inspired by the simplicity of curves and forms of the human body. Opposite: Athlete Jacqui Agyepong, photographed by Herb Ritts for TAG Heuer in 1997.

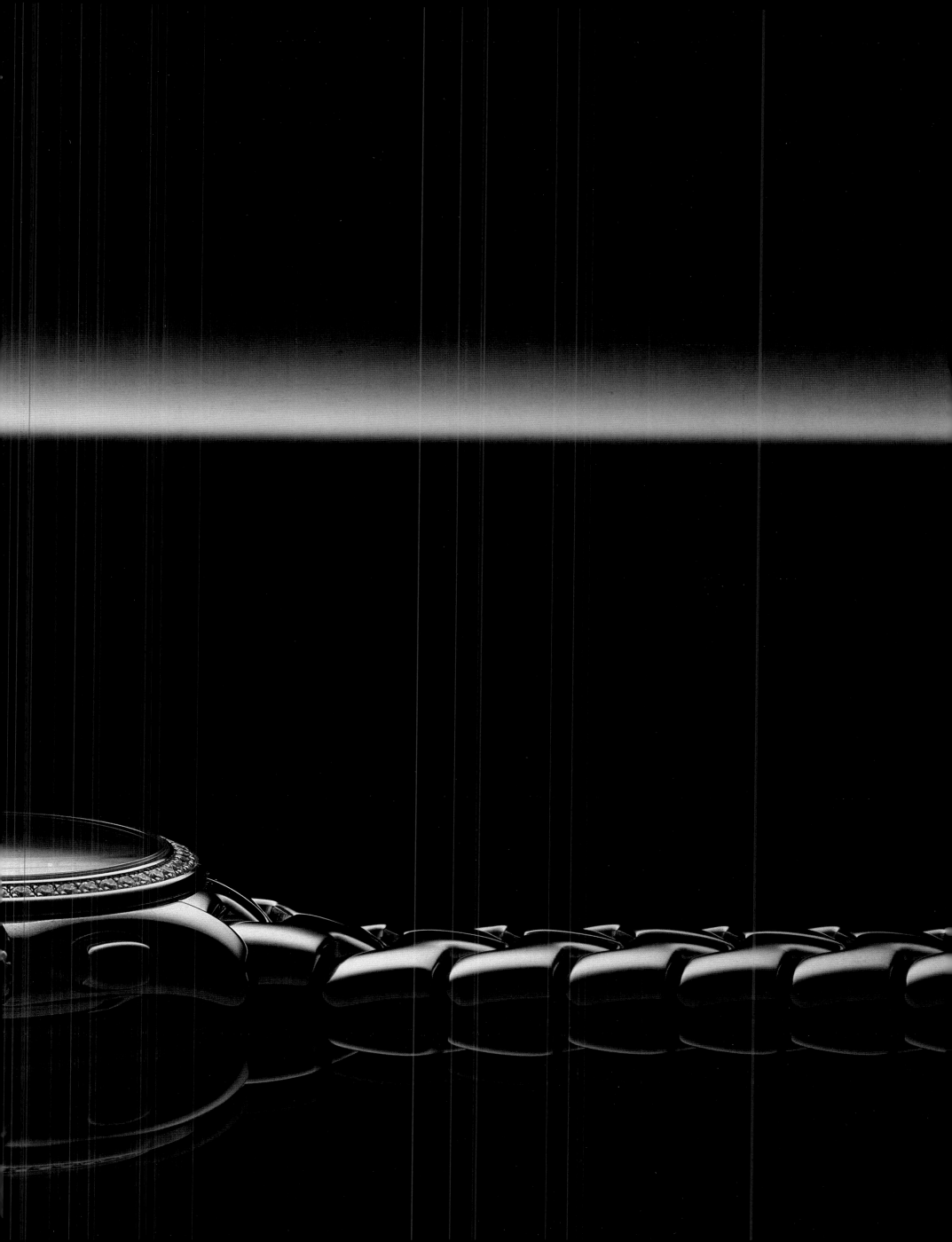

Grace and character. Previous pages: Link DDDB (Diamond Dial Diamond Bezel) chronograph for women, 2008.
This page: TAG Heuer Grand CARRERA Calibre 6 RS.

Power lines. The TAG Heuer MERIDIIST capitalizes on the company's ability to fashion an object that will be in constant proximity to the body.

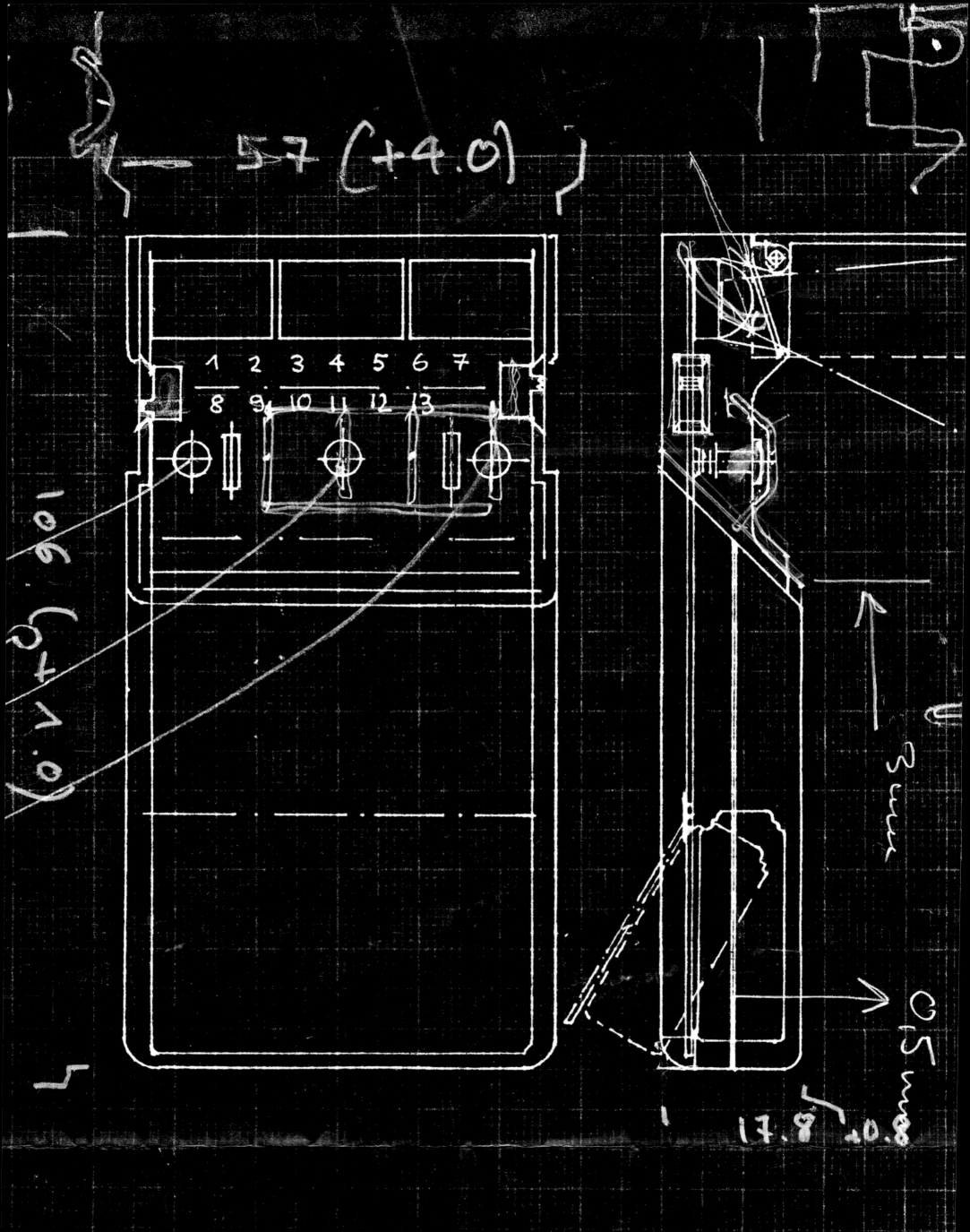

Timeless design. This page: The Microsplit LCD 320.
Opposite: Technical drawings for the Microsplit LED 520, both designed in 1976 by Richard Sapper.

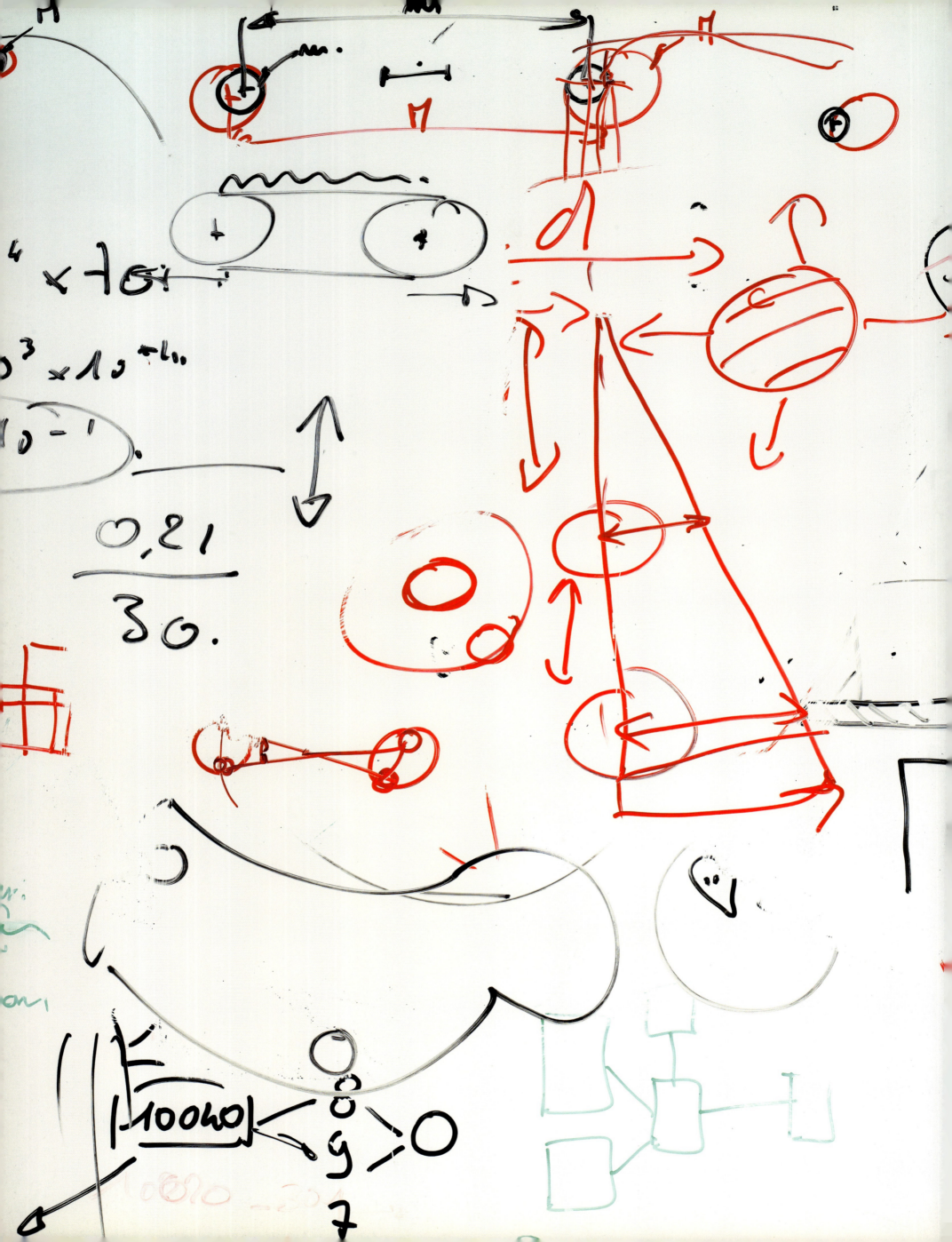

> "If at first the idea is not absurd, then there is no hope for it."
>
> **Albert Einstein**

Opposite: Monaco V4 technical brainstorming board.

Geometric shapes. This page: Stairs in steel and frosted glass at TAG Heuer headquarters.
Opposite: TAG Heuer's "SKIN" booth at Baselworld 2007.

sometimes a straight line breaks all the rules.

> **"Genius is personal, decided by fate, but it expresses itself by means of system. There is no work of art without system."**

Le Corbusier
architect

Taking a strong angle. Previous page: The Monaco *Sixty Nine*, 2003. Opposite: Corbusier's Villa Shodan, Ahmedabad, India, 1956.

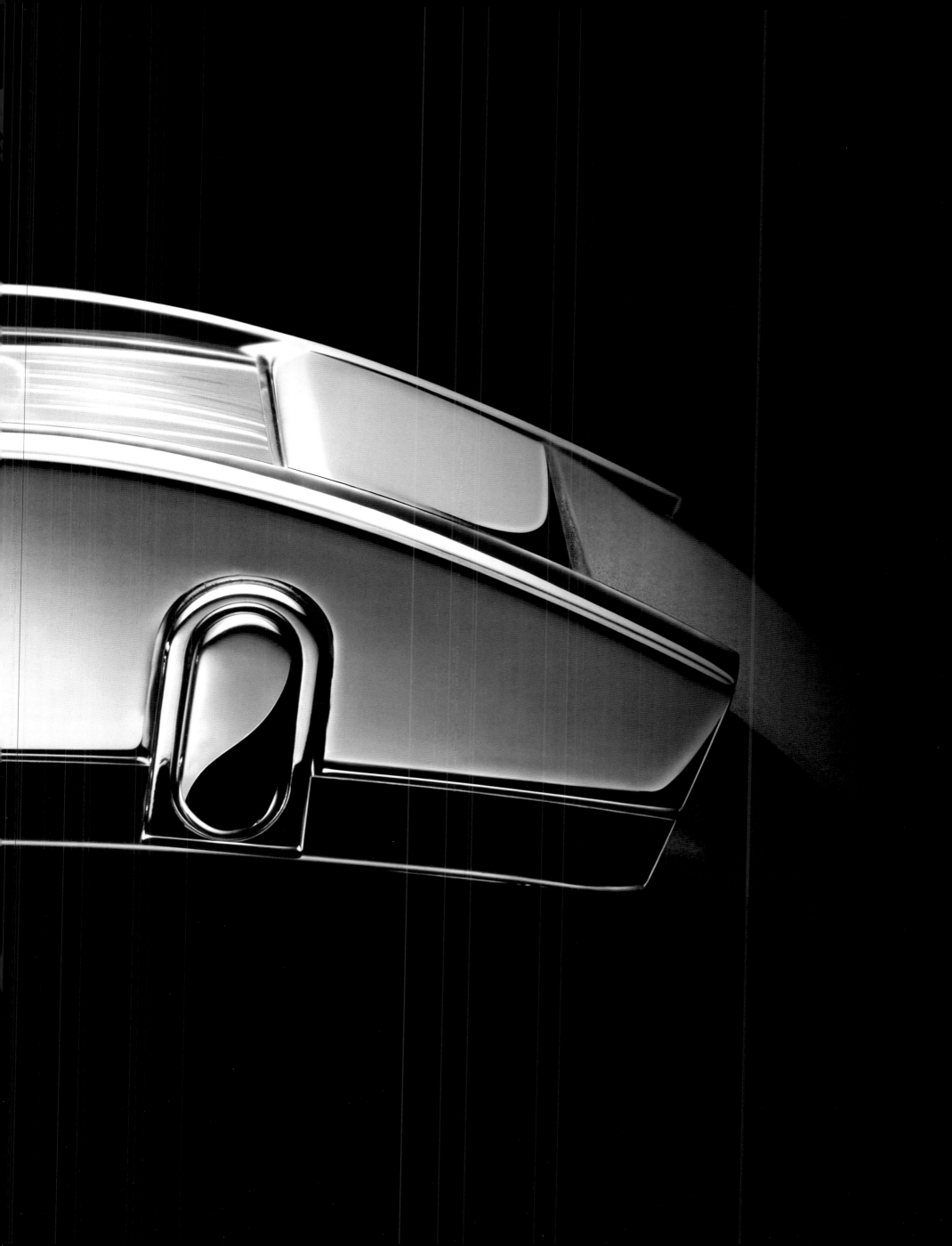

Unique technology and fluid design.
Previous page: The Micrograph F1, an authentic wrist-worn sport timing instrument accurate to 1/100th of a second.
This page: Black rubber strap of the TAG Heuer Carrera Calibre 1.

Curves ahead. Previous page: The Honestino Guimarães National Museum by Oscar Niemeyer, Brasilia. This page: TAG Heuer Avant-Garde Eyewear, Curve series. Following pages: *Le commencement du monde*, ca. 1920, Constantin Brancusi. Photographed by the artist. Musée national d'art moderne, Paris.

Creativity is an unknown lar

guage everyone understands.

Flexible lines. This page: The TAG Heuer Grand CARRERA Calibre 36 RS2 Caliper Chronograph Ti2.
Opposite: Bernar Vernet, *Ligne indéterminée*, 1996, rolled steel. Private collection.

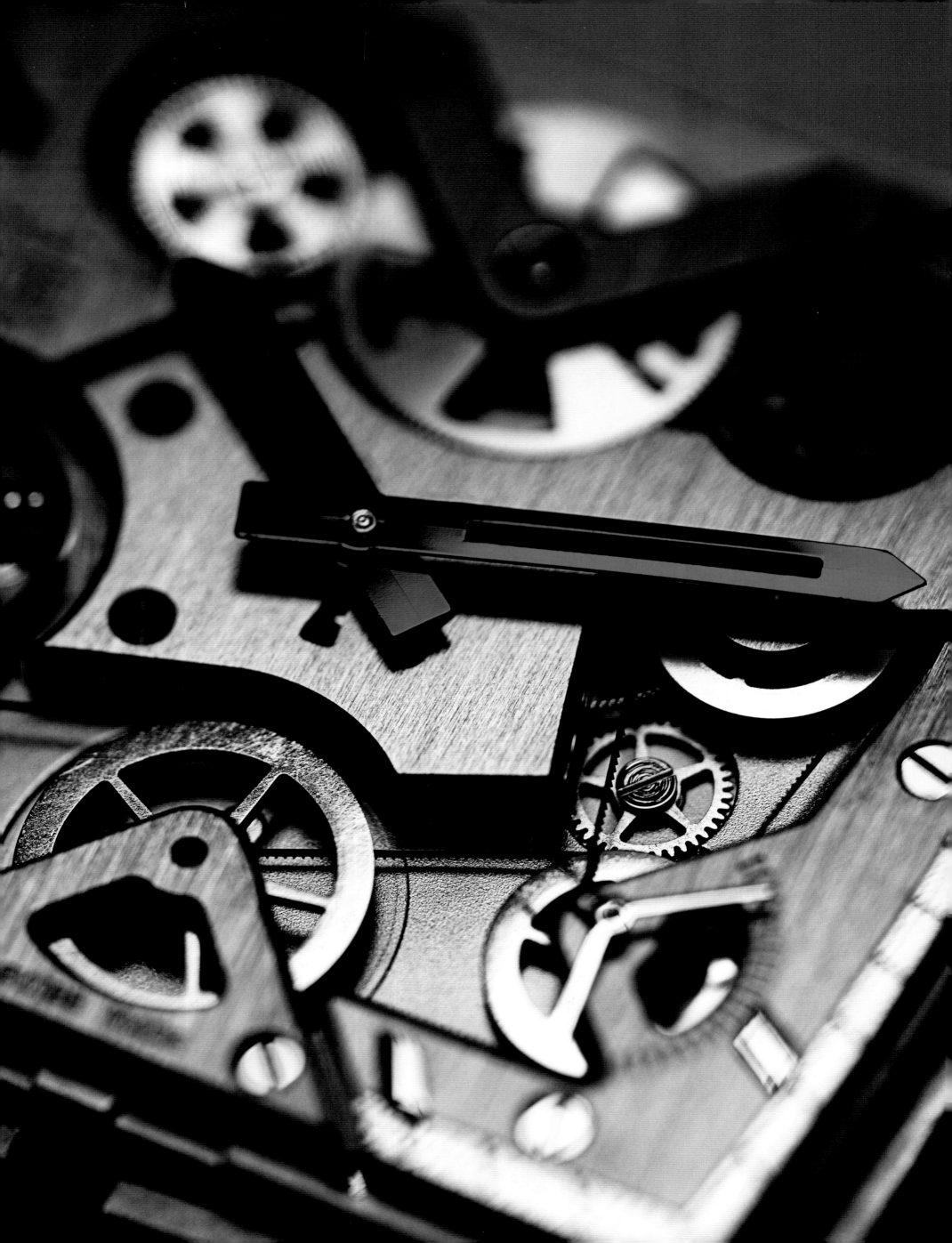

Driving force. This page: Engine of a car. Opposite: The Monaco V4, the world's first watch with belt transmission system directly inspired by a car engine's design. First unveiled as a concept watch at Baselworld in 2004, it went into production in 2009.

Modern geometry. This page: The Chronosplit Manhattan GMT, 1977.
Opposite: The IAC Building in New York, designed by Frank Gehry, 2007.

Symmetry. This page: Olympic high-diving champion Marjorie Gestring, 1936. Opposite: Skyscraper by Oscar Niemeyer and Lucio Costa, 1960.

"Day after day, determination hones the body of an athlete. A natural sculpture fashioned by the will to win. Form determined by function."

Christoph Behling
designer

Form. Opposite: The Swiss athlete Anita Weyermann, photographed by Herb Ritts for TAG Heuer in 1997. As the 1996 Junior World Champion, she was the first to win three gold medals at the same championship.

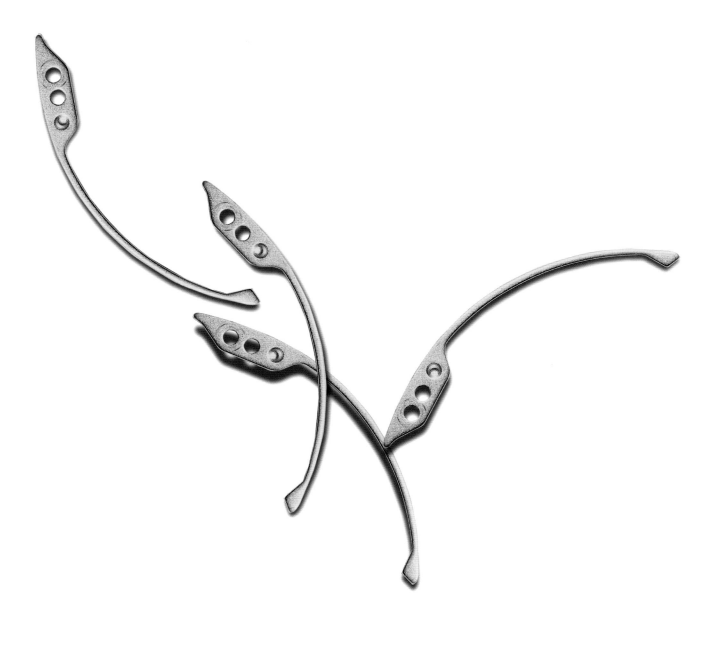

Compositions. This page: Column-wheel jumper, a component of the Calibre 11, Calibre 12, Calibre 14, and Calibre 15.
Opposite: *Lunatique neonly 16 quarts de cercle n°2*, 2001, François Morellet, Collection Wurth.

Ergonomic design. The Professional Golf Watch, 2005.

Man of steel. This page: Vintage Heuer strap in black PVD. 1000 series. Opposite: Track star Colin Jackson, TAG Heuer Ambassador from 1998 to 2000, photographed by Herb Ritts for TAG Heuer in 1998.

> "When you're racing, it's life. Anything that happens before or after is just waiting."

Steve McQueen
in the film *Le Mans*

In the spotlight. MONACO 40th anniversary re-edition Automatic Chronograph Calibre 11 Limited Edition, 2009, a stunning tribute to the original Monaco worn by Steve McQueen in while filming the classic racing movie *Le Mans*.

Elegant proportions. This page: TAG Heuer AQUARACER 500M CALIBRE 5.
Opposite: TAG Heuer building, La Chaux-de-Fonds, Switzerland.

Futuristic design. The McLaren Technology Centre in Woking, U.K., designed by renowned architect Sir Norman Foster.

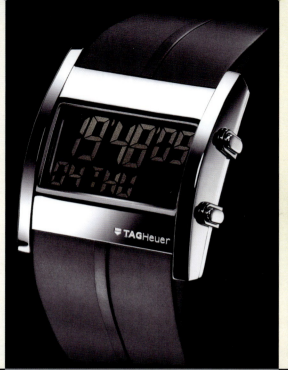

The Knights of Time.

Success. It's a mind game. This was the slogan that accompanied one of the most striking advertising campaigns of the 1990s, articulating TAG Heuer's understanding that life is a race, and that often the biggest challenge an individual will face is mental. This sense of being locked in competition with oneself was explained through a set of compelling visual metaphors: a swimmer pursued by sharks in a pool, relay racers handing over a baton of burning dynamite, a hurdler clearing a giant razor blade, a sailing yacht tacking away from the edge of a deadly waterfall, and a show jumper urging his mount to leap from one skyscraper to another.

This underlying sense of TAG Heuer wearers seeking to exceed perceived limits comes from their dedication to grueling training regimens that will yield those vital tenths, hundredths, and thousandths of a second that mark the difference between winning and simply taking part. But these attributes are perhaps most obviously demonstrated by the sports personalities who, over the years, have played a crucial part in the TAG Heuer story. The tenacity, dedication, moral strength, and mental endurance demonstrated by sports stars are also common to individuals who find success and fulfillment in other spheres. And it is this similarity that led to the provocative campaign asking, "What are you made of?" Just as Edouard Heuer laid down a challenge to time itself when he set out to create the best chronographs he was capable of, so today TAG Heuer challenges all of us to look inside and become our best possible selves.

The men and women who wear TAG Heuer refuse to acknowledge the limits that hold others back. Move. Change. Evolve. Adapt. These are the verbs that fuel their restless drive, powering them to surge forward on a tide of ambition, to move beyond the mundane and the mediocre. The will to succeed ignites in these people the desire to improve, outdistance, and outpace. Winning and losing, failure and success, weakness and strength—these are life's teachers. These are the values of the people at TAG Heuer. These are the values of TAG Heuer Ambassadors Tiger Woods, Maria Sharapova, Leonardo DiCaprio, Steve McQueen, and Lewis Hamilton. For these people, there is no finish line. They were surely all born with talent, but it is their hard work and superior mental strength, like that of TAG Heuer master watchmakers, that allows them to distinguish themselves the way they do. They are pioneers. To them, these qualities are more than values; they represent a way of life. Though all of them are leaders, they never cling to victory. For them the reward is the struggle. Forget mere awards and empty trophies. What pushes TAG Heuer, and the exceptional men and women who represent the brand, to greatness is not recognition and laurels but something inside, unseen and deep in their souls.

Think of Tiger Woods dropping a long putt, or Lewis Hamilton slicing out of the slipstream and accelerating through a curve. Think of the kinetic beauty of Maria Sharapova as she shifts direction in midstride and hits an impossible forehand out of her backhand corner. On the screen, it's even more apparent. What an actor like Leonardo DiCaprio is made of is visible in every frame.

But it's not only visible in those moments of sporting and artistic epiphany. It's the entire arc of exceptional lives. Every dream. Every obstacle. Every sacrifice. These are the stanzas in the epic poem of life. To merge together these moments, we must power past the mundane and the mediocre toward an ever-renewing idea of perfection. We must have the mettle to overcome, reinvent, challenge, and evolve, to transcend obstacles to realize dreams, to attain the unattainable—and then to keep going, setting our sights ever higher, visualizing horizons as yet unmapped. This is what TAG Heuer is made of.

Le Massif, Québec, Canada, at -30° C.

> Many drivers are consistently fast, but only a very few have the mental energy to push themselves to the limit.

Jo Siffert, the first TAG Heuer Ambassador, between 1969 and 1971.

The name TAG Heuer immediately c
Whether one is a sports enthusiast or
logo sweeps us into the dynamic world

jures up visions of Formula One races.
ply keen on precision, the TAG Heuer
of competition and speed.

" Time means possibility. What we choose to do with that time is up to us, but hopefully, we'll make the right choices, responsible choices that help lead to a better future for the next generation."

Leonardo DiCaprio

Leonardo DiCaprio, TAG Heuer Ambassador since December 2008, photographed by Tom Munro for TAG Heuer.

"Stick to your guns and know what you want."

Kristin Scott Thomas

Kristin Scott Thomas, TAG Heuer Ambassador in 1999 and 2000, photographed by Peter Lindbergh for the launch of the Alter Ego series.

When you you get to you your top physical performance, you understand that

> "I was the third-youngest and the first Russian player to win Wimbledon. Making sacrifices, making history. It made me who I am today."

Maria Sharapova

Maria Sharapova, TAG Heuer Ambassador since 2005, photographed by Tom Munro for TAG Heuer.

The real race

has no finish line.

> "I'm not sure whether I'm an actor who races, or a racer who acts."

Steve McQueen

Steve McQueen in *The Thomas Crown Affair*, 1968.
Following pages: Close-up of Steve McQueen's eyes.

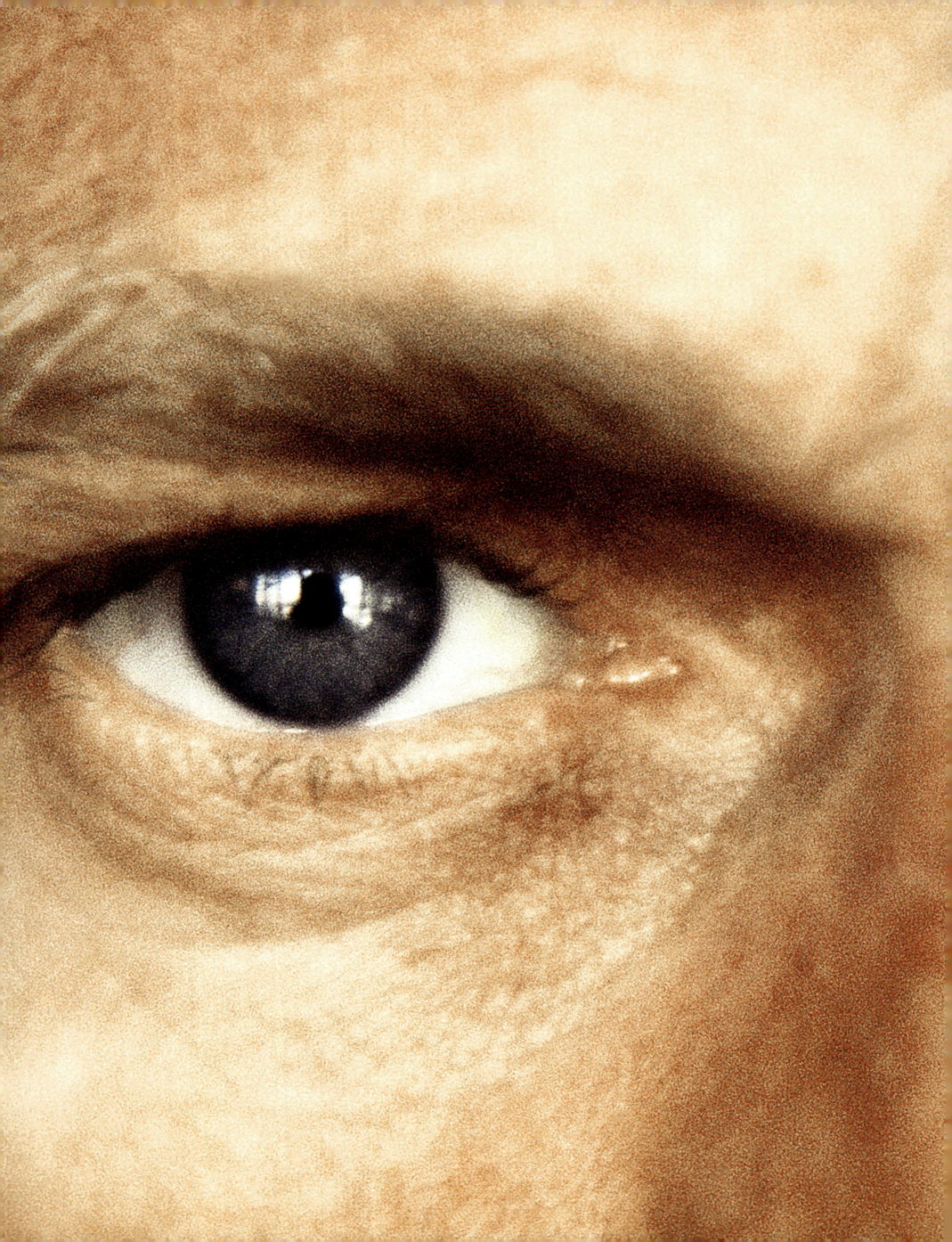

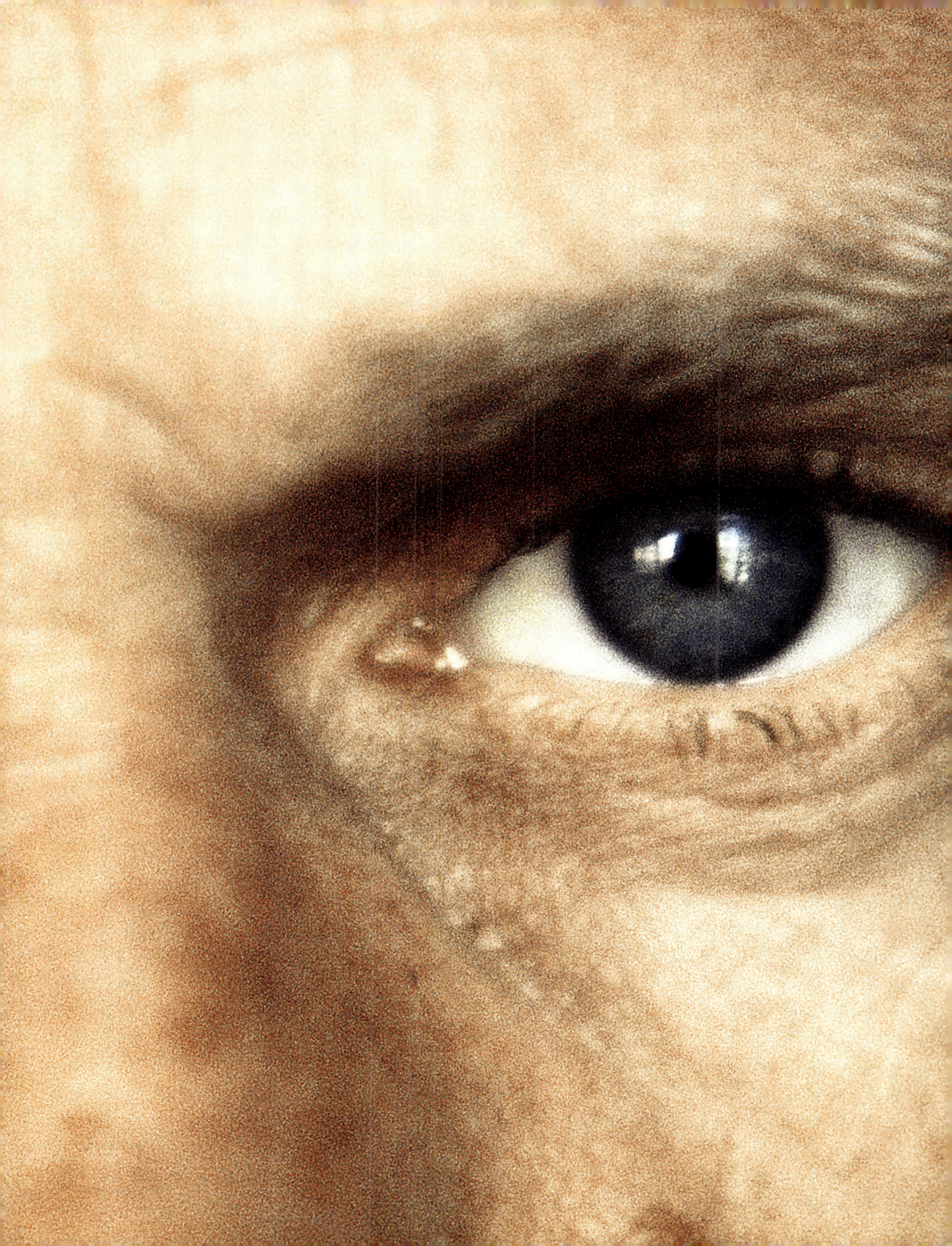

"When you are on the line and there are eight great athletes on the line, it does all boil down to strength of the mind, the will of the body, and the way you're gonna go and determine what's going to happen in the end."

Colin Jackson

Colin Jackson, track athlete, TAG Heuer Ambassador from 1998 to 2000, photographed by Anton Corbijn for the TAG Heuer campaign "Inner Strength."

No setback i

> **"** My obsession
> is producing
> exceptional timepieces. **"**

Denis Badin
TAG Heuer watchmaker,
Meilleur Ouvrier de France

The greater the risk, the higher the reward.

Juan Manuel Fangio arrived first in a Mercedes-Benz 300 at the World Championship of Sports Car Brands during the Swedish Grand Prix in Kristianstad, August 7, 1955.

"Whatever sport you do, if you really want to win, you can do it.**"**

Kimi Räikkönen

Kimi Räikkönen, TAG Heuer Ambassador since 2005 and 2007 Formula One world champion.

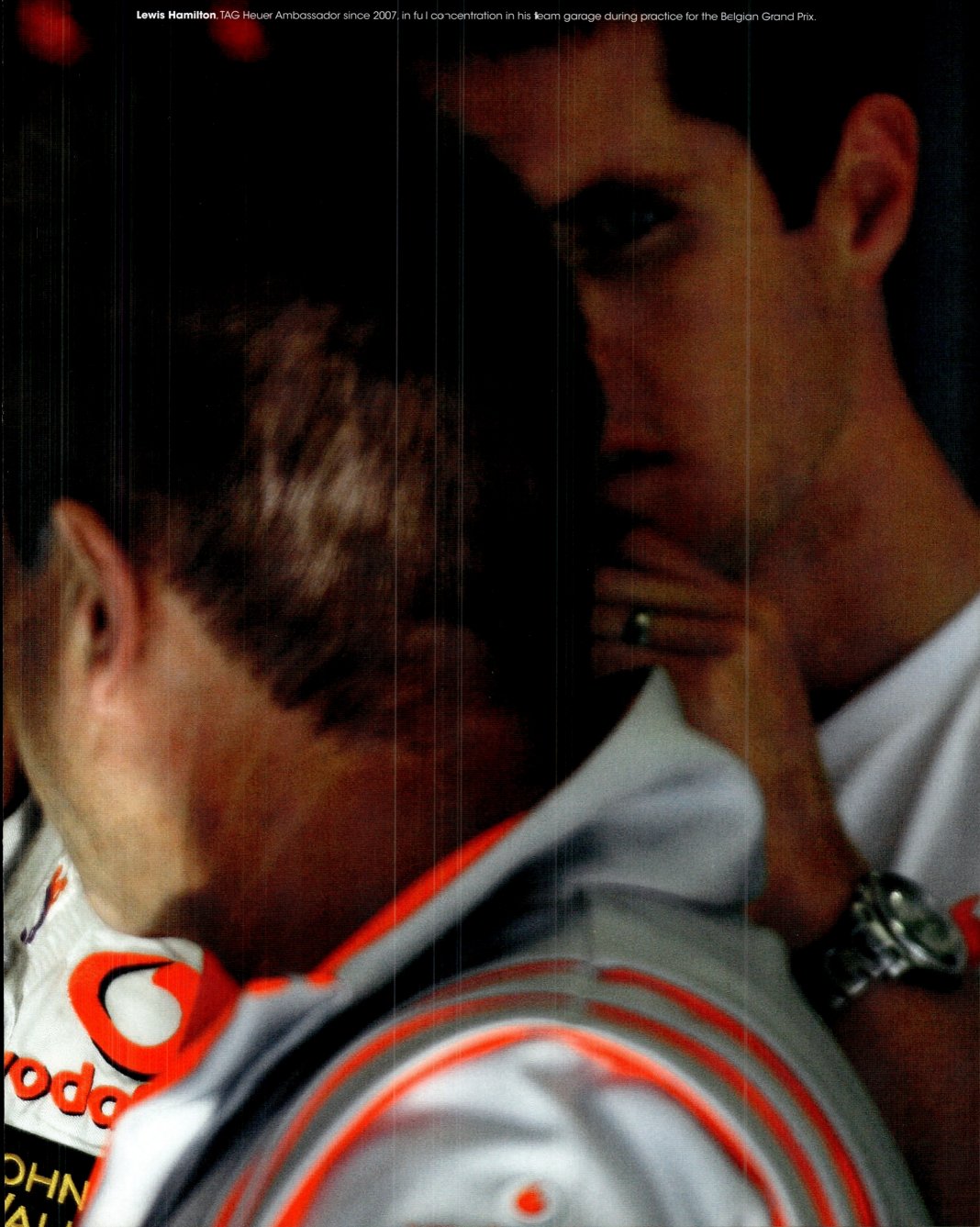
Lewis Hamilton, TAG Heuer Ambassador since 2007, in full concentration in his team garage during practice for the Belgian Grand Prix.

24 Heures du Mans. Starting line of the race in 1969.

Ayrton Senna moments before the departure of the Italian Grand Prix in 1990.

> **"No matter how far behind or how much I'm down. I refuse to quit. Quitting is not an option."**
>
> **Tiger Woods**

Tiger Woods, TAG Heuer Ambassador since 2003, photographed by Tom Munro for TAG Heuer.

China Team, sponsored by TAG Heuer, during the 32nd America's Cup, 2007.

The difference between those who aspire to success and those who do succeed is not physical, it is metaphysical; it is not a difference of sight, but of vision.

> **"Since I was very young, I had decided I wanted to be a Formula One champion.... It was guts and hard work that made it possible. Every day I had to push myself."**
>
> **Lewis Hamilton**

Lewis Hamilton, TAG Heuer Ambassador since 2007, photographed by Tom Munro for TAG Heuer.

> "We learn by looking back, but we will only achieve by looking forward."
>
> **Barack Obama**

"Time never stops. Why should we?"

Jack Heuer

Jack Heuer, great-grandson of Edouard Heuer and honorary president of TAG Heuer since 1999.

Acknowledgments

I would like to pay a special tribute to:

Jack Heuer and his family, for building and conserving the heritage of the company;

Jean Campiche, Jean-Jacques Racine, and Jeff Stein, for their knowledge of watches and the history of our brand, as well as their assistance in the compiling of this book;

Past and current TAG Heuer Ambassadors Jacqui Agyepong, Leonardo DiCaprio, Lewis Hamilton, Colin Jackson, Kimi Räikkönen, Maria Sharapova, Kristin Scott Thomas, Anita Weyermann, and Tiger Woods, for adding glamour and prestige to the brand and for helping us to be where we are today;

Christoph Behling, Richard Sapper, and the TAG Heuer watchmakers, whose expert hands and ideas have developed and molded exceptional timepieces;

Photographers Bèla Adler & Salvador Fresneda, Joël von Allmen, Adrian Gaut, Albert Giordan, Marco Grob, Laziz Hamani, Russell & Connie Guzman, Peter Lindbergh, Tom Munro, and Herb Ritts, whose pictures have made this book a true art creation;

Constantin Brancusi, Sir Norman Foster, Frank Gehry, Le Corbusier, François Morellet, Oscar Niemeyer, and Bernar Venet, the artists and architects who have trusted us with their knowledge and passion to enabled us to express our vision of the world;

Philippe Siffert, Chadwick McQueen and the Terry McQueen Testamentary Trust, the Instituto Ayrton Senna, the Juan Manuel Fangio Museum, and the Archives of Bienne, for their useful cooperation and contributions;

The whole TAG Heuer team, for its endless pioneering spirit and commitment;

And you, the reader, who is helping to continue our legacy.

Jean-Christophe BABIN
President & CEO, TAG Heuer

The publisher would like to thank Françoise Bezzola, Mathilde Tournois, Elodie Metra, Isabelle Ducat, Charles Fritscher, Kay Guttmann, Sarah P. Hanson, Nelly Riedel, Véronique Ristelhueber, Valérie Tougard, and Meredith Mendelsohn & Brad Randlett of Affordable Translations for their efforts and considerable support in the making of this book.

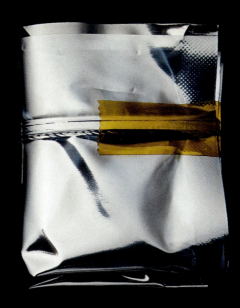
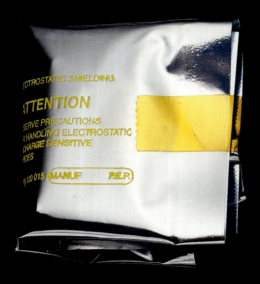

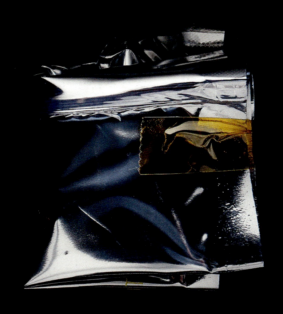
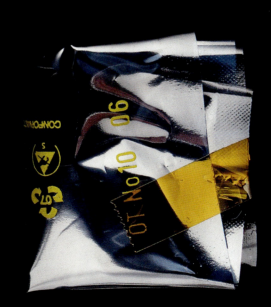

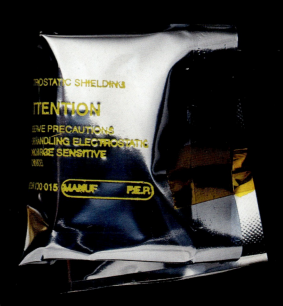

Photo credits

Front Endpaper-P. 1 © Ministère de la culture - France/AAJHL/Jacques Henri Lartigue
P. 2-3 © Schlegelmich/Corbis
P. 4-5 © Michel Comte
P. 6-7 © ASE/photo Norio Koike
P. 14 TAG Heuer archive
P. 15 © Joël von Allmen
P. 16-23 TAG Heuer archive
P. 24-25 © Albert Giordan
P. 26 © Ministère de la culture-Médiathèque du Patrimoine-Dist. RMN/Art Resource, NY
P. 27 TAG Heuer archive
P. 28 © Albert Giordan
P. 29-31 TAG Heuer archive
P. 32 © Roger-Viollet
P. 33-34 TAG Heuer archive
P. 35 TAG Heuer archive/All rights reserved.
P. 36-39 TAG Heuer archive
P. 42 © Maurice Tabard/All rights reserved.
P. 41-42 © TAG Heuer archive
P. 43 © Getty/Hulton Archive
P. 44 The Kobal Collection
P. 45-46 TAG Heuer archive
P. 47 © Rue des Archives
P. 48-49 TAG Heuer archive
P. 50-51 © Albert Giordan
P. 52-53 TAG Heuer archive
P. 54-55 TAG Heuer archive/All rights reserved.
P. 56-57 © Nicolas Boon
P. 58 © Getty
P. 59 © Tom Munro for TAG Heuer
P. 60-61 © Eveline Perroud for TAG Heuer

P. 65-67 © Laziz Hamani
P. 68 © Jacques Vekemans/Gamma
P. 69 © Joël von Allmen
P. 70 © TAG Heuer archive
P. 71 © Joël von Allmen
P. 72-73 © Michael Jansson
P. 74-75 © Pierre Vallet
P. 75 TAG Heuer archive/All rights reserved.
P. 77 © Laziz Hamani
P. 78 © Jacques Vekemans/Gamma
P. 79 TAG Heuer archive/All rights reserved.
P. 80-81 © Laziz Hamani
P. 82-83 © Mark Thompson/Getty
P. 85 © Laziz Hamani

P. 86-89 TAG Heuer archive/All rights reserved.
P. 90-91 © Laziz Hamani
P. 92-93 © Jacques Vekemans/Gamma
P. 94-95 © Laziz Hamani
P. 96 © Gérard Vandystadt
P. 97 © Albert Giordan
P. 98 © Claude Sculnier/DPPI
P. 99 © Christoph Behling
P. 100 © Joël von Allmen
P. 101 © Laziz Hamani

P. 105 © Joël von Allmen
P. 106 © David Zaccharias
P. 107 © Herb Ritts
P. 108-109 © Laziz Hamani
P. 110-112 © Joël von Allmen
P. 113 © Adrian Gaut
P. 114 TAG Heuer archive
P. 115 © Albert Giordan
P. 116 © Laziz Hamani
P. 118 © Adrian Gaut
P. 119 TAG Heuer archive
P. 120-121 © Joël von Allmen
P. 123 © Lucien Hervé/Artedia and © Artists Rights Society (ARS, New York/ADAGP, Paris
P. 124 © Luc Boegly/Artedia
P. 125 © Anderson & Low
P. 126-127 © Joël von Allmen
P. 128 © Bèla Adler and Salvador Fresneda
P. 129 © Laziz Hamani
P. 130-131 © Nick Clements
P. 132-133 Archives Lego and TAG Heuer/All rights reserved.
P. 134-135 © CNAC/MNAM/Dist. RMN/Art Resource, NY and © Artists Rights Society (ARS), New York/ADAGP, Paris
P. 136 © Laziz Hamani
P. 137 © Archives Bernar Venet/New York and © Artists Rights Society (ARS), New York/ADAGP, Paris
P. 138 © Laziz Hamani
P. 139 © Corbis
P. 140 © Albert Giordan
P. 141 © Adrian Gaut
P. 142 John Gutmann/Collection Center for Creative Photography, University of Arizona © 1998 Arizona Board of Regents
P. 143 © René Burri/Magnum Photos

P. 145 © Herb Ritts
P. 147 © Archives François Morellet and © Artists Rights Society (ARS) New York/ADAGP, Paris
P. 148-149 TAG Heuer archive/All rights reserved.
P. 150 © Laziz Hamani
P. 151 © Herb Ritts
P. 152 © Joël von Allmen
P. 154 © Adrian Gaut
P. 155 © Joël von Allmen
P. 156-157 © The McLaren Group
P. 158-159 © Joël von Allmen

P. 162-163 TAG Heuer archive/All rights reserved.
P. 164-165 TAG Heuer archive/All rights reserved.
P. 166-167 © Harry Gruyaert/Magnum Photos
P. 168-169 © Tom Munro for TAG Heuer
P. 171 © Peter Lindbergh
P. 172-173 © Russell & Connie Guzman (from a campaign by BDDP for TAG Heuer)
P. 174-175 © Tom Munro for TAG Heuer
P. 176-177 TAG Heuer archive/All rights reserved.
P. 179 Collection Christophe L.
P. 180-181 © Getty
P. 183 © Anton Corbin
P. 184-185 © Michael Jansson
P. 186 © Jacques Vekemans/Gamma
P. 188-189 © The Fangio Foundation and Mercedes Benz
P. 191 © Marco Grob
P. 192-193 © Getty
P. 194-195 © DPPI
P. 196-197 © ASE/photo Norio Koike
P. 198-199 © Tom Munro for TAG Heuer
P. 200-201 © DPPI
P. 202-203 © Russell & Connie Guzman (from a campaign by BDDP for TAG Heuer)
P. 204-205 © Arno Minkkinen
P. 206-207 © Tom Munro for TAG Heuer
P. 208 © Raymond Depardon/Magnum Photos
P. 211 © Joël von Allmen
P. 212 © Laziz Hamani
P. 214 © Laziz Hamani

Pages 49, 60, 181, 182, 183: Steve McQueen™ Licensed by Chadwick McQueen and the Terry McQueen Testamentary Trust, represented by GreenLight, LLC, as Corbis Corporation.

© 2009 Assouline Publishing
601 West 26th Street, 18th floor
New York, NY 10001, USA
Tel.: 212 989-6810 Fax: 212 647-0005
www.assouline.com

ISBN: 978 2 75940 412 4

Text by Nick Foulkes
Graphic Design: Isabelle Ducat
Color separation by Planète-Couleurs (France)
Printed by Grafiche Milani (Italy)

No part of this book may be reproduced in any form
without prior permission from the publisher.

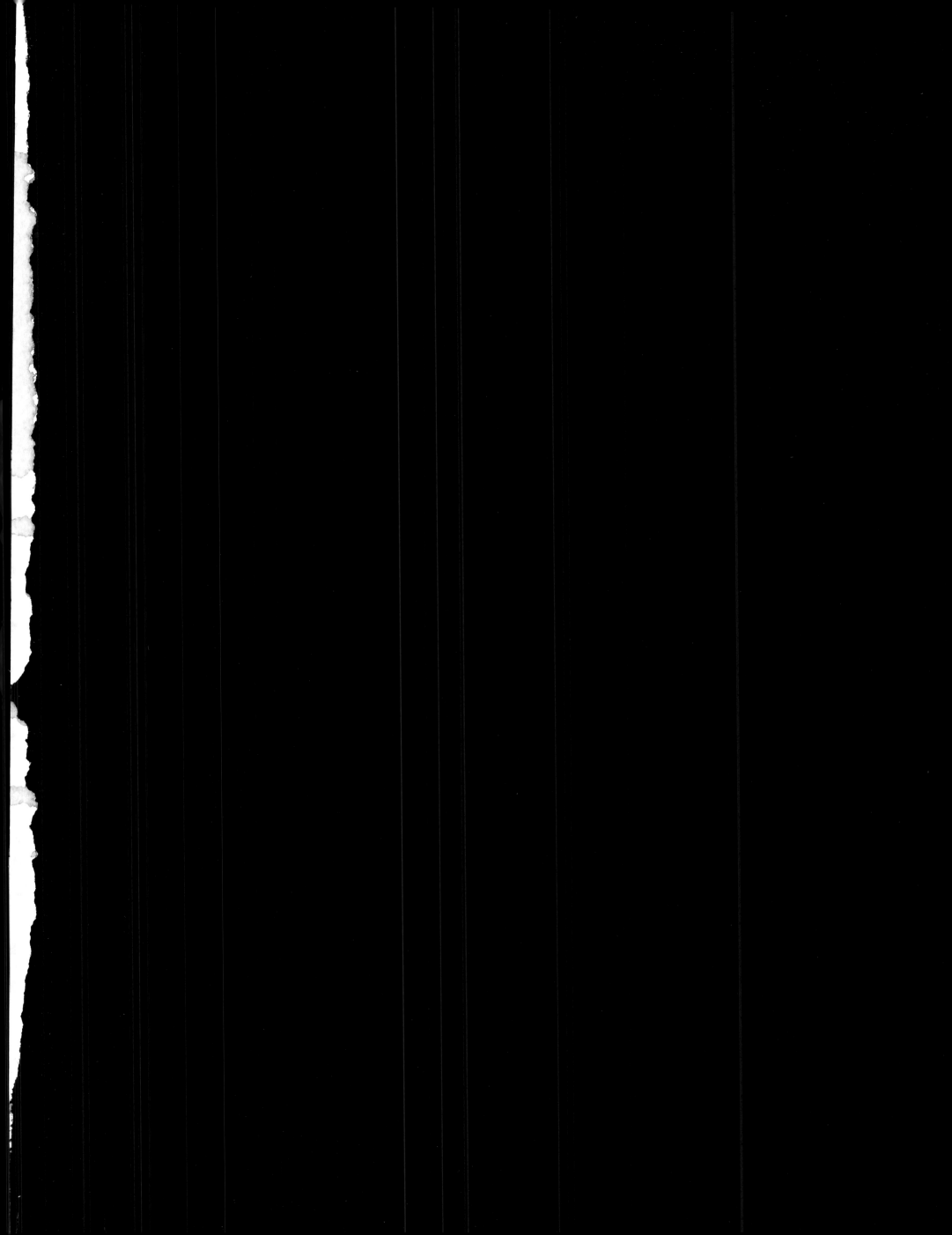

The most beautiful stor

Page 14, Line 3, Column 3, Page 16, Line 1, Column 5, Page 19, Line 1, Column 3 and Line 3, Column 2: Artedia/Artists Rights Society (ARS), New York/Pictoright, Amsterdam. Page 14, Line 1, Column 3, Page 14, Line 3, Column 2: Artedia/Artists Rights Society (ARS), New York/SABAM, Brussels. Page 13, Line 3, Column 5: Artists Rights Society (ARS), New York/Pictoright, Amsterdam. Page 14, Line 1, Column 4, Page 19, Line 1, Column 1: Courtesy Cheim & Read, NY. Page 6, middle right: Adriano Cimarosti. Page 15, Line 4, Column 4: Corbis. Page 18, Line 1, Column 2, Esto. Page 12, Line 3, Column 2: Khatrine. Page 7, middle left. Page 12, Line 1, Column 3. Page 15, Line 3, Column 3: Peter Knapp. Page 17, Line 1, Column 3 and Line 3, Column 5: Page 18, Line 1, Columns 4 and 5. Page 19, Line 3, Columns 4 and 5: Getty. Page 5, Page 12, Line 2, Column 4. Page 17, Line 2, Column 3: François Halard. Page 15, Line 1, Column 2: Jamie Brady/Artifice Images. Page 19, Line 1, Column 3 and Line 3, Column 5. Page 18, Line 1, Columns 4 and 5. Page 19, Line 3, Columns 4 and 5: Getty. Page 5, Page 12, Line 2, Column 4. Page 17, Line 2, Column 3: François Halard. Page 15, Line 1, Column 1: Magnum. Page 12, Line 1, Column 1: Museum of Modern Art, NY. Page 15, Line 1, Column 2: Maywald/Artists Rights Society (ARS)/Bono, Oslo. Page 14, Line 3, Column 1. Page 17, Line 1, Column 4, Column 4: Magnum. Page 12, Line 1, Column 1: Museum of Modern Art, NY. Page 15, Line 1, Column 2: Maywald/Artists Rights Society (ARS)/Bono, Oslo. Page 14, Line 3, Column 1. Page 17, Line 1, Column 4, Knapp. Page 17, Line 1, Column 5. Page 13, Line 1, Column 3: Roger-Viollet. Page 11, Line 3, Column 2: Artists Rights Society (ARS)/Bono, Oslo. Page 14, Line 3, Column 1. Page 17, Line 1, Column 4, NASA. Page 10, Line 1, Column 3. Page 11, Line 1, Column 5. Page 13, Line 1, Column 2: Artists Rights Society (ARS), New York/ADAGP, Paris. Page 11, Line 1, Column 4. Page 13, Line 3, Column 3. Page 14, Line 1, Column 1. Column 5. Rue des Archives/Artists Rights Society (ARS), New York/ADAGP, Paris. Page 12, Line 3, Column 1: Stedelijk Museum, Amsterdam. Page 7 left: Gérard Vandystadt. Page 16, Line 1, Column 4. Page 17, Line 3, Column 2: Vitra.

Translated by Leah Brumer (from French)

> 1995 > 1996 > 1997 > 1998 > 1999

HISTORIC, CULTURAL, AND SCIENTIFIC EVENTS

Strong earthquake causes serious damage in Kobe, Japan.
Musée d'art Moderne de la Ville de Paris pays tribute to **Louise Bourgeois.***

"Mad cow" epidemic threatens British herds.
Analysis of a meteorite from Mars reveals the possibility of life on other planets.
Olympic Games held in Atlanta.

Ceremony marking the return of **Hong Kong to China** is held.
Dolly, the first cloned mammal, is born.
Guggenheim Museum* in Bilbao, designed by architect Frank Gehry, is inaugurated.

The **iMac*** is introduced, marking Apple's rebirth.
McLaren Mercedes team, featuring Mika Häkkinen, wins the Formula One constructors' and drivers' world championship.

The **single European currency** takes effect.
Bertrand Piccard and Brian Jones make the **first nonstop, around-the-world balloon flight.** They travel 42,810 kilometers in 19 days, 1 hour, and 49 minutes.

HEUER AND TAG HEUER

The advertising campaign **"Success. It's a Mind Game,"*** is launched.
TAG Heuer participates in the **Louis Vuitton Cup** and the **America's Cup** with Chris Dickson and the TAG Heuer Challenge.

The famous TAG Heuer **Carrera*** chronograph is reissued.
TAG Heuer becomes a public company.

TAG Heuer launches the **Kirium** series with the support of a remarkable team of athletes, photographed by **Herb Ritts**.

Monaco* series reissued in a limited edition of 5,000.
The **2000 Classic, 2000 Exclusive, and 2000 Searacer** series are introduced.

The **S/el** series is renamed **Link** and its design changes.
2000 Sport series and a new line cedicated exclusively to women, **Alter Ego**, are launched.
The Alter Ego line features prominent spokeswomen, including **Monica Seles** and **Kristin Scott Thomas**.
TAG Heuer joins the **LVMH group (Moët Hennessy Louis Vuitton)**, the world's leader in luxury goods.
TAG Heuer is the Official Timekeeper of the **World Ski Championship** in Vail, Colorado.

> 2005 > 2006 > 2007 > 2008 > 2009

HISTORIC, CULTURAL, AND SCIENTIFIC EVENTS

Kyoto Protocol takes effect.
World population is estimated at 6.5 billion.
Fondation de la Haute Horlogerie is created.

First face transplant performed in France.
Musée du quai Branly* opens in Paris, designed by architect Jean Nouvel.

Airbus A380 makes its first commercial flight.
Driver **Kimi Räikkönen is the Formula One world champion.**
Seventh and final volume of J. K. Rowling's **Harry Potter** series is published.

Summer Olympic Games held in Beijing.
Vodafone McLaren Mercedes driver Lewis Hamilton wins the FIA world championship.*
World's tallest tower, the Burj Dubai, is inaugurated.

Barack Obama* is sworn in on January 20, 2009. The new president of the United States has worn a TAG Heuer 1500 watch since the 1990s.

HEUER AND TAG HEUER

The **Calibre 360 Concept Chronograph**, the first mechanical wrist chronograph accurate to 1/100th of a second, is introduced.
The first **Professional Golf Watch***, developed in collaboration with Tiger Woods, is launched.
The concept watch Diamond Fiction earns the Grand Prix d'Horlogerie de Genève in the Ladies Watches category.
TAG Heuer taps Uma Thurman, Brad Pitt, Maria Sharapova, Kimi Räikkönen, and Juan Pablo Montoya as new brand ambassadors.
TAG Heuer is an official partner of the China Team in the **America's Cup**.

The **Monaco Calibre 360 LS*** concept chronograph is introduced.
The **TAG Heuer Carrera Calibre 360** Rose Gold Limited Edition, winner of the Grand Prix d'Horlogerie de Genève Sports Watches, is launched.
TAG Heuer clocks a **2/10,000th-of-a-second gap** between the two winners of the **Race of Champions Nations' Cup**.

TAG Heuer launches the **TAG Heuer Grand CARRERA** with Calibre RS, the first mechanical movement engineering with Rotating Systems.
Link Calibre S and **Aquaracer Calibre S Regatta**, chronographs with electromechanical movement, are launched. The Aquaracer wins the Popular Science "Best of What's New" award.
New booth, **TAG Heuer SKIN***, inaugurated at Baselworld.
Lewis Hamilton and Fernando Alonso join Kimi Räikkönen as TAG Heuer ambassadors.

The **TAG Heuer Grand CARRERA Calibre 36 RS Caliper Concept Chronograph***, the first automatic chronograph capable of displaying 1/10ths of a second, featuring the Caliper rotating scale, is introduced.
Its honors include the **Grand Prix d'Horlogerie de Genève** in the Sports Watches category.
TAG Heuer opens its **TAG Heuer 360 Museum**.
TAG Heuer joins the Fondation de la Haute Horlogerie (FHH).
TAG Heuer launches the **MERIDIIST** luxury mobile phone and accessories.
TAG Heuer Avant-Garde Eyewear's C-Flex concept receives a SILMO Golden Award.

For the **Monaco's 40th anniversary**, TAG Heuer reissues the first blue **Monaco Calibre 11** in a limited edition of 1,000 pieces, introduces the **Monaco Twenty Four Concept Chronograph** and launches the **Aquaracer 500M Calibre 5**.
TAG Heuer's Baselworld booth wins a Silver Award in EXHIBITOR magazine's 23rd Annual Exhibit Design Awards competition.
The famous **"What Are You Made Of?"** advertisements are relaunched.
The campaign includes new TAG Heuer brand ambassador **Leonardo DiCaprio.***

1990 > 1991 > 1992 > 1993 > 1994 >

HISTORIC, CULTURAL, AND SCIENTIFIC EVENTS

1990: Germany reunifies. The Gulf War begins. Nelson Mandela is freed. Gorbachev receives the Nobel Peace Prize. The **McLaren team, featuring Ayrton Senna, wins the Formula One constructors' and drivers' world championship.**

1991: CERN, the European Center for Nuclear Research, announces its **World Wide Web. McLaren Mercedes and Ayrton Senna win the Formula One constructors' and drivers' world championship.** Rem Koolhaas builds the Villa dall'Ava in Saint Cloud.*

1992: **The United Nations Conference on the Environment and Development** is held in Rio de Janeiro, Brazil. The **Maastricht Treaty** is signed, creating the European Union. Winter Olympic Games held in Albertville and summer Olympic Games held in Barcelona.

1993: British, Soviets, and Americans suspend nuclear testing. Russian cosmonauts Anatoly Solovyev and Sergei Avdeyev return to Earth after a 189-day flight on the *Mir* space station.*

1994: Nelson Mandela* is elected president of South Africa. The tunnel under the English Channel is inaugurated. **Brazilian Formula One driver Ayrton Senna dies at the Imola course.**

HEUER AND TAG HEUER

The **1500***, 4000, and Super 2000 series are introduced.

The **"Don't Crack Under Pressure"*** ad campaign, featuring Ayrton Senna and Michael Schumacher, is introduced. TAG Heuer is the Official Timekeeper for the **Indianapolis Motor Speedway.**

The **6000** series is introduced. The FIA, the International Automobile Federation, selects TAG Heuer as the **Official Timekeeper for the Formula One World Championship (1992–2003).**

TAG Heuer sponsors the renowned French skipper, **Titouan Lamazou**, in the Jules Verne Trophy regatta. **Mika Häkkinen*** joins McLaren and becomes a TAG Heuer ambassador.

TAG Heuer introduces the **6000** in **18-karat solid gold** at its new booth at the World Watch and Jewelry Show in Basel.

2000 > 2001 > 2002 > 2003 > 2004 >

HISTORIC, CULTURAL, AND SCIENTIFIC EVENTS

2000: Transition to the year 2000 goes smoothly, despite **Y2K** fears.

2001: **September 11 attacks** occur in the U.S. **Tiger Woods wins the Masters.** He is the first golfer to win four Grand Slams in a row. Apple launches the iPod.*

2002: **World Summit on Sustainable Development** held in Johannesburg, South Africa. Winter Olympics held in Salt Lake City. Roman Polanski presents his film *The Pianist* in Warsaw.

2003: **The war in Iraq begins.** Space shuttle *Columbia* disintegrates while re-entering the Earth's atmosphere. Construction ends on the 345-meter long *Queen Mary 2* cruise ship.

2004: The **Taipei 101 tower*** is completed in Taiwan. Zaha Hadid receives the Pritzker Prize for Architecture.

HEUER AND TAG HEUER

The **Kirium Ti5***, the first watch made of a polished titanium alloy, Ti5, from the McLaren Formula One team, is launched. **Jean-Christophe Babin** becomes president and CEO of TAG Heuer.

The **Kirium Formula 1**, a modern analog watch with a digital chronograph accurate to 1/100th of a second, is introduced. **The Monza*** is reissued and the **Link Searacer** is launched. **Jack Heuer** becomes honorary president of TAG Heuer. TAG Heuer is the **Official Timekeeper of the World Ski Championships in St. Anton, Austria.**

The **Micrograph F1**, a digital chronograph accurate to 1/100th of a second, wins the **Grand Prix d'Horlogerie de Genève in the Design Watches category**. **Targa Florio, Monza Calibre 36** and **Link Calibre 36** are launched, all accurate to 1/10th of a second. **Sportvision sunglass line** introduced. TAG Heuer ambassadors David Coulthard, Zhang Ziyi, Inés Sastre, and Steve McQueen are featured in the brand's new ad campaign, **"What Are You Made Of?"***

The **2000 Aquagraph** and the **Microtimer***, a timekeeping instrument for the wrist accurate to 1/1,000th of a second, are launched. **Autavia is reissued.** TAG Heuer is the **Official Timekeeper for the World Ski Championships in St. Moritz** and sponsors the Oracle BMW Racing team in the Louis Vuitton Cup and America's Cup. No. 1 golfer **Tiger Woods** becomes a TAG Heuer Ambassador.

The concept watch **Monaco V4***, with a belt-driven mechanical movement, and the **TAG Heuer SLR chronograph for Mercedes-Benz**, are introduced. The 2000 series becomes the **Aquaracer**. Introduced in 2003, the **Monaco Sixty Nine**, the first reversible chronograph watch with two kinds of movement and accurate to 1/1,000th of a second, wins the **Grand Prix d'Horlogerie de Genève in the Design Watches category**. TAG Heuer is the **Official Timekeeper of the Indy Racing League** and the renowned **Indianapolis 500**.

* pictured

> 1974 > 1975 > 1976 > 1977 > 1978

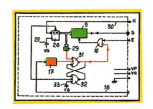

McLaren and Emerson Fittipaldi win the Formula One constructors' and drivers' world championship. Roland Moreno invents the smart card.*

Suez Canal reopens after eight years. Two manned spaceships— the *Apollo*, an American craft, and the *Soyuz*, a Soviet—meet in space.* **The Ferrari racing team and Niki Lauda earn the Formula One constructors' and drivers' world championship.**

Winter Olympic Games held in Innsbruck.* Summer Olympic Games held in Montreal. **Ferrari team wins the Formula One constructors' world championship.**

Ferrari racing team and Niki Lauda earn the Formula One constructors' and drivers' world championship. George Lucas' film *Star Wars* is released. Georges Pompidou Centre* in Paris, designed by Richard Rogers and Renzo Piano, opens.

Quartz watches outstrip mechanical ones in popularity, causing one of Switzerland's most serious watch crises. First child conceived in vitro is born in Great Britain. **Ferrari driver Niki Lauda wins the Formula One world championship again.**

HISTORIC, CULTURAL, AND SCIENTIFIC EVENTS

Silverstone* chronograph is introduced. Heuer also sponsors the McLaren Formula One team. **Record year for Heuer-Léonidas, with sales above 26 million Swiss francs.** Charles-Edouard Heuer dies.

Chronosplit LED/LCD*, accurate to within 1/10th of a second, is introduced. **Monza** chronograph is launched.

The Daytona, the Regatta, the Chronosplit LCD, accurate to within 1/100th of a second, and the **Microsplit LCD***, a pocket quartz timing instrument accurate to within 1/100th of a second and designed by **Richard Sapper**, are introduced.

Chronosplit Manhattan GMT*, the first quartz bracelet chronograph with both analog and digital displays, accurate to within 1/100th of a second, is launched. The **Kentucky, Jarama,** and **Cortina** chronographs are introduced, and the **Split Lap Unit 77** digital chronograph is designed for Ford.

Heuer presentes the **1000 series***, the first quartz diver watch, water-resistant up to 200 meters. Introduces the **Senator** and **Verona** series.

HEUER AND TAG HEUER

> 1985 > 1986 > 1987 > 1988 > 1989

Mikhail Gorbachev becomes president of the U.S.S.R. Reagan and Gorbachev meet at the Geneva summit. Robert D. Ballard discovers the wreck of the *Titanic*. **The McLaren team and Alain Prost win** the Formula One constructors' and drivers' world championship.

The Chernobyl disaster occurs. **Alain Prost wins the Formula One world championship.** Musée d'Orsay opens in Paris. Ron Arad designs the Well-Tempered Chair.* Fuji introduces the disposable camera.

Gorbachev pursues *glasnost* ("opening") and *perestroika* ("rebuilding"). Construction begins on the **Channel tunnel**. Jean Nouvel and Architecture Studio finish building the Arab World Institute in Paris.

Winter Olympic Games held in Calgary and summer Olympic Games held in Seoul. **McLaren wins the Formula One constructors' world championship.** The **Louvre Pyramid***, designed by Ieoh Ming Pei, is inaugurated.

The fall of the Berlin Wall* marks the symbolic end of the Cold War. **The McLaren Mercedes stable and Alain Prost win the Formula One constructors' and drivers' world championship.**

HISTORIC, CULTURAL, AND SCIENTIFIC EVENTS

Titanium, Airline, and **Executive** series, and the **125th-anniversary collection,** are introduced. Heuer joins the TAG Group (Techniques d'Avant-Garde) and becomes **TAG Heuer.*** The company sponsors skipper Mike Birch and his catamaran, the *Formule TAG*, the first Kevlar®-and-carbon-fiber catamaran. **TAG Heuer and McLaren Mercedes begin the longest partnership in Formula One history.**

TAG Heuer Formula 1* series, combining steel and glass fiber, is launched. TAG Heuer enters the skiing World Cup, sponsoring French and Austrian skiers Marc Girardelli, Helmut Höflehner, and others.

The **S/el*** (sport/elegance) series is introduced. The **"Six Features"** advertising campaign is launched.

The **Tristar** series is launched. **McLaren driver Ayrton Senna*** becomes TAG Heuer's ambassador. TAG Heuer and **Carl Lewis** sign a sponsorship contract in September.

The 1/100th-of-a-second chronograph version of the S/el series is launched. TAG Heuer is the Official Timekeeper for the **Alpine Ski World Cup** in the U.S. and Canada.

HEUER AND TAG HEUER

1969 > 1970 > 1971 > 1972 > 1973 >

HISTORIC, CULTURAL, AND SCIENTIFIC EVENTS

On July 21, Neil Armstrong becomes the first man to walk on the moon. Concorde* makes its maiden flight. The forerunner of the Internet is developed, spurred by the U.S. Department of Defense. Development of the heavy-cargo transport plane, the Boeing 747, is completed.

The VCR is introduced. People's Republic of China launches its first satellite. Shiro Kuramata designs the Revolving Cabinet.*

China becomes a member of the U.N. Médecins Sans Frontières (Doctors Without Borders) is established. **U.S.S.R. develops the first manned space station.** ATM machine introduced.*

First U.N. conference on the environment held in Stockholm. Olympic Games held in Munich. Richard Sapper creates the Tizio lamp.*

Watergate scandal breaks in the U.S. **Israeli-Palestinian conflict produces first oil-price shock.** World Trade Center opens in New York. Alexander Solzhenitsyn publishes *The Gulag Archipelago*. The Sydney Opera House* is inaugurated.

HEUER AND TAG HEUER

The **world's first automatic chronograph movement with a micro rotor, the Chronomatic Calibre 11,** is introduced. The **Monaco***, the world's first chronograph with a square, water-resistant case, is introduced. Well-known Swiss race-car driver **Jo Siffert** wears Heuer chronographs and becomes the company's first official ambassador.

Steve McQueen* wears a **Monaco** chronograph and racing overalls with the Heuer logo in the film *Le Mans*, directed by Lee H. Katzin. On April 24, Heuer-Léonidas SA issues **4,000 shares** (nominal value of 250 Swiss francs) at a price of 925 Swiss francs. **Jack Heuer** becomes CEO.

Calculator* and **Easy-Rider** chronographs are introduced. Heuer is the **Ferrari** racing team's Official Timekeeper until 1979, and drivers **Clay Regazzoni** and **Jacky Ickx** wear the company logo on their overalls. Swiss ski team uses Heuer chronographs.

Heuer creates the **Le Mans Centigraph**, an electronic chronograph accurate to 1/1,000th of a second, for the Ferrari racing team. Launch of the **Montreal** and **Temporada** chronographs and the **Microsplit 800*** chronographs, the world's first pocket quartz-timing instrument. Heuer products are exported to 102 countries.

Heuer launches the **Microsplit 820**, the world's first pocket quartz timing instrument accurate to 1/100th of a second.

1979 > 1980 > 1982 > 1983 > 1984 >

HISTORIC, CULTURAL, AND SCIENTIFIC EVENTS

Philips and Sony develop the compact disc.* **The Ferrari racing team, with Jody Scheckter, wins the Formula One world championship constructors' and drivers' title.**

Test launches of the European rocket, *Ariane*, begin. CNN, the first continuous news network, starts broadcasting. Ettore Sottsass creates the Memphis Milano Italian design group.*

Airbus A310 and Boeing 757 make their first flights.

Prof. Luc Montagnier identifies the AIDS virus. Sanyo introduces the first consumer VHS camera in Japan. Richard Marquand's *Return of the Jedi*, the sixth and final *Star Wars* film, is released.

Space shuttle *Discovery* makes its first flight. Norman Foster builds headquarters for the Hongkong & Shanghai Bank.*

HEUER AND TAG HEUER

Pasadena series is launched.

As part of the Swiss Timing organization, Heuer is the Official Timekeeper at the winter Olympics in Lake Placid and the summer Olympics in Moscow. During a state visit to Switzerland, **Spanish king Juan Carlos*** congratulates Jack Heuer on the company's products.

2000* series is launched. The new **Lémania SA** acquires all Heuer-Léonidas SA shares, preserving the brand and Heuer-Léonidas jobs.

The **Golden Hours series** of 18-karat gold prestigious watches and chronographs for collectors is launched.

1000 M professional diver's watch, **3000***, and **Pilot** series are launched.

*pictured

> 1946 > 1947 > 1948 > 1949 > 1955

American rocket travels 88 km.
Mass production of the **Volkswagen Beetle*** begins.
E. Piaggio manufactures the Vespa scooter.
First Cannes Film Festival is held.

Willard F. Libby develops carbon-14 dating.
Charles Yeager achieves first supersonic speed in a rocket plane.
Dior creates the New Look.*

United Nations adopts the Universal Declaration of Human Rights.
First vinyl records introduced.*
Auguste Piccard develops first diving machine, the bathyscaphe.
Winter Olympic Games held in St. Moritz and Summer Olympic Games held in London.

NATO formed.
German Democratic Republic and Federal Republic of Germany are established.
In 1953, **the first civilian jet plane, the Comet***, begins regular flights to Australia.
Two-stage American rocket reaches altitude of 402 kilometers.

Warsaw Pact signed.
First McDonald's restaurant opens in the U.S.
Le Corbusier's Notre-Dame-du-Haut chapel is built in Ronchamp.*
Beatnik movement born in California.

HISTORIC, CULTURAL, AND SCIENTIFIC EVENTS

General Eisenhower purchases a second Heuer chronograph.

Heuer launches production of **automatic wristwatches.***
Prince Wilhelm of Sweden and Harry S. Truman both wear a gold Heuer chronograph.

Heuer introduces the **Auto-Graph***, a wrist chronograph watch with a tachymeter scale and a hand that can be preset manually.
Receives first Desco orders from Japan.

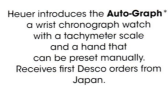

Launch of the **Solunar**, the first watch equipped with a tide indicator.
One thousand pieces are produced.
The chronograph **Mareograph***, featuring a tide level indicator and countdown function, is introduced afterwards and only launched in 1950.
This model is called the **Seafarer** in the U.S.

Patent obtained for the **Twin-Time***, a GMT watch that displays the time in two zones simultaneously.
Heuer provides 3 stopwatches accurate to within 1/10th second for the third South Georgia Survey.

HEUER AND TAG HEUER

> 1964 > 1965 > 1966 > 1967 > 1968

Summer Olympic Games are held in Tokyo and winter Olympic Games in Innsbruck.
Sailor Éric Tabarly breaks the world record for a solo crossing of the Atlantic.
Donald Campbell reaches a speed of 648.72 km/hour in his turbine-powered automobile.
Richard Sapper and Marco Zanuso design the TS 502* radio for Brionvega.

Muhammad Ali becomes heavyweight world champion.
In his jet-propelled car, the *Spirit of America*, Craig Breedlove breaks the world's land speed record, achieving a speed of 996.57 km/hour.
Gae Aulenti designs the Pipistrello lamp.*

Cultural Revolution begins in China.
Soviets' *Luna 9* spacecraft lands safely on the moon and transmits televised images.
André Courrèges's* structured white garments are a fashion success.

The Six-Day War breaks out in the Middle East.
Christiaan Barnard conducts the first heart transplant.
Francis Chichester concludes the world's first around-the-world solo sail.
Arthur Penn's film *Bonnie and Clyde* is released.

**Martin Luther King, Jr. is assassinated.
Students revolt in America, Japan and Europe.**
Athletes at the Olympic Games in Mexico give the Black Power salute.
Stanley Kubrick's film *2001: A Space Odyssey* is released.*

HISTORIC, CULTURAL, AND SCIENTIFIC EVENTS

Heuer launches the **Heuer Carrera* chronograph.**
Heuer and Léonidas merge, creating **Heuer-Léonidas SA**.
Sales figures double.

Innovation introduced in the Heuer Carrera model:
the world's first bracelet chronograph with digital date display printed on a rotating disc.

Heuer obtains a patent for the **Microtimer, the first miniaturized, electronic sports timer accurate to 1/1,000th of a second.**

The *Intrepid* and its skipper, Emil Mosbacher, win the **America's Cup** with **Heuer chronographs** on board.

Autavia GMT is introduced.
The wrist chronograph features a rotating bezel for second time zone.
Heuer designs a chronograph* for **Bundeswehr** pilots (the army of the Federal Republic of Germany).
Camaro chronograph is launched.
Heuer-Léonidas receives a major order for calibre Valjoux 7700 from China and the U.S.

HEUER AND TAG HEUER

1935 > 1936 > 1939 > 1942 > 1945 >

HISTORIC, CULTURAL, AND SCIENTIFIC EVENTS

1935: Huge, 313-meter ocean liner *SS Normandie* makes first transatlantic crossing. **Howard Hughes* sets a new world-aviation speed record, reaching 530 km/hour.** George Gershwin presents his first opera, *Porgy and Bess*. Nylon fiber invented in the U.S.

1936:  The Winter Olympics are held in Garmisch-Partenkirchen; the Summer Games in Berlin. The *Queen Mary* ocean liner makes her maiden voyage. **Frank Lloyd Wright designs Fallingwater* in Pennsylvania.**

1939: **WWII begins.** Germany attacks Poland. World's Fair* held in New York. Victor Fleming's film *Gone With the Wind* is released.

1942:  First uranium fission chain reaction. **The atomic era is born at 3:30 p.m. CST on December 2.** Peggy Guggenheim* opens gallery in New York.

1945: **Yalta Conference held.** General surrender ends war on the European front. **United Nations and UNESCO are created.** Atomic bombs dropped on Hiroshima and Nagasaki; Japan surrenders.

HEUER AND TAG HEUER

1935:  Heuer develops **chronograph for pilots** with a turning bezel.

1936: Jules Jürgensen brand is sold. Company returns to former name, **Ed. Heuer & Cie.**

1939:  Heuer chronographs chosen by Committee of the **National Exhibition in Zurich**. Company introduces **water-resistant wrist chronograph.***

1942: Heuer includes a **warranty** with all chronographs sold in Switzerland.

1945:  Heuer introduces **triple calendar** (day, date, and month) **chronograph**. All Heuer products signed on the movement, dial, and case. **General Dwight D. Eisenhower*** purchases a Heuer chronograph with a steel case.

1957 > 1958 > 1959 > 1962 > 1963 >

HISTORIC, CULTURAL, AND SCIENTIFIC EVENTS

1957:  **Treaty creating the European Economic Community (EEC) is signed.** Diving depth record of 1,122 meters is set. Albert Camus receives the Nobel Prize for Literature. **Soviets send the first *Sputnik** into space.**

1958: Brussels World's Fair features the Atomium*, a monument forming the shape of a unit cell of an iron crystal. **An atomic submarine reaches the North Pole.** Pop music is born in England. Ingvar Kamprad opens the first Ikea store in Sweden.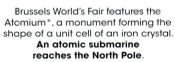

1959:  The **Vietnam war** begins. **Fidel Castro** takes power in Cuba. A Soviet rocket reaches the moon. **First computer processor is built in the U.S.** Kilby seeks patent for a silicon-based semiconductor integrated circuit. The Guggenheim Museum*, designed by Frank Lloyd Wright, opens in New York.

1962: The 315-meter *SS France*, the world's largest passenger ship, is launched. **Yves Saint Laurent presents his first collection.*** John Steinbeck receives the Nobel Prize for Literature. The Rolling Stones hold their first concert.

1963:  **U.S. president John F. Kennedy is assassinated.** Martin Luther King Jr. gives his "I Have A Dream" speech. The "red telephone" connecting the U.S. and the U.S.S.R. is set up. Alfred Hitchcock's film *The Birds** is released.

HEUER AND TAG HEUER

1957:  Heuer launches the **Ring-Master stopwatch***, a world first that features seven interchangeable rings with scales that can be adapted to time various sports. **Prince Bertil of Sweden** wears it the following year.

1958: 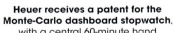 **Heuer receives a patent for the Monte-Carlo dashboard stopwatch**, with a central 60-minute hand and a 12-hour jumping disc. Together with the 8-day **Master-Time** dashboard clock, the pair is called the **Rally-Master**. Heuer redesigns the **Auto-Rallye** dashboard stopwatch and launches the **Super-Autavia** dashboard chronograph. **Jack Heuer***, Charles-Edouard's son, joins the company.

1959:  Heuer launches the **Game-Master***, a wrist stopwatch for radio, television, and film directors. **Heuer Time Corporation** is established in the U.S.

1962: **Autavia* wrist chronograph** introduced. Astronaut John Glenn wears a **Heuer sport wrist stopwatch** as he orbits the Earth three times on board the spaceship *Mercury Friendship 7*. Heuer is the first Swiss watch in space.

1963:  Heuer launches the **Film-Master*** stopwatch, which allows Hollywood directors to measure and track 16- and 35-millimeter film sequences. The **Sebring**, a dashboard stopwatch with a split-second hand, is introduced.

*pictured

> 1913	> 1914	> 1915	> 1916	> 1919	
 Stainless steel discovered. **New York's Grand Central Terminal***, world's largest train station, opens. Marcel Duchamp produces his first readymade, *Bicycle Wheel*. Coco Chanel opens her couture house in Paris.	**WWI** begins. Panama Canal* opens. Airplane-height record of 8,150 meters is set. 	Albert Einstein develops his general theory of relativity. Alexander Samuelson develops first Coca-Cola bottle.* 	The Dadaist movement officially born on February 8 in Zurich.	The Treaty of Versailles signed. **League of Nations founded in Geneva.** First Paris–London commercial flight. Bauhaus* founded in Weimar. 	HISTORIC, CULTURAL, AND SCIENTIFIC EVENTS
 **Heuer publishes first newspaper advertisement.**	 **First Heuer bracelet chronographs** appear, featuring a Valjoux 15 calibre movement with a crown at 12 o'clock.	Patent for shock-resistant case (26328). **Charles-Edouard Heuer***, Charles-Auguste's oldest son, joins company after two years of training. 	 Charles-Auguste Heuer invents **first sports stopwatches accurate to 1/100th of a second, the Mikrograph and the Microsplit*** (with split-seconds), followed by the **Semikrograph and the Semicrosplit** (with split-seconds), accurate to 1/50th of a second.	**The Zeppelin R 34**, with a **Time of Trip** on board, makes the first flight over the North Atlantic. 	HEUER AND TAG HEUER

> 1929	> 1930	> 1931	> 1933	> 1934	
Wall Street crashes on October 24 ("Black Thursday"). **Sixteen competitors participate in first Monaco Grand Prix.** New York Museum of Modern Art founded. Ludwig Mies van der Rohe creates the Barcelona* furniture line. 	 The first World Cup soccer game is held in Uruguay. Josef von Sternberg's film *The Blue Angel** and Luis Buñuel and Salvador Dalí's film *Age of Gold* are released.	Harold Eugene Edgerton develops electronic flash for photography. Pierre Chareau builds the Glass House.* 	Roosevelt launches the New Deal and abolishes prohibition. Hitler becomes chancellor of the German Reich. **Malcolm Campbell's*** automobile reaches a speed of **407 kilometers/hour.** Aviator Wiley Post circles the earth in 121 hours. 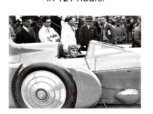	 Gerrit Rietveld creates the Zig-Zag* chair. Olympic champion Johnny Weissmuller hired to play Tarzan on film.	HISTORIC, CULTURAL, AND SCIENTIFIC EVENTS
Heuer logo takes final form.* Graf Zeppelin carrying **Hugo Eckener** on a record-setting around-the-world trip (20 days, 4 hours) is equipped with a Heuer Time of Trip. 	**A watertight case for bracelet watches** is produced.	The city of Bienne presents **Prof. Auguste Piccard*** with a gold Heuer chronograph with a 17-line movement to commemorate his flight into the stratosphere with Bienne physicist Paul Kipfer. 	**The Autavia***, the first dashboard instrument for racecars, and **Hervue***, featuring a movement that does not need to be wound for 8 days, are launched. 	 Ed. Heuer & Co. participates in the **Swiss Watch Fair in Basel** for the first time, presenting a wide range of sports stopwatches, chronographs, and dashboard watches.	HEUER AND TAG HEUER

1907 > 1908 > 1910 > 1911 > 1912 >

HISTORIC, CULTURAL, AND SCIENTIFIC EVENTS

1907

Five-car automobile race from Beijing to Paris is held. Cubism is born when Picasso completes his painting *Les Demoiselles d'Avignon.**

1908
Olympic Games held in London. **Ford issues the Model T*, the first low-priced, mass-produced automobile**. First movie studio founded in Hollywood.

1910

International railway system reaches 1 million kilometers. Architect Adolf Loos builds the Steiner House of reinforced concrete in Vienna.

1911
Marie Curie receives Nobel Prize in Chemistry for discovering radium and polonium. **American engineer Frederick Winslow Taylor lays foundation for the scientific organization of work (OST) with his book *The Principles of Scientific Management*.** Roald Amundsen is first person to reach the South Pole.

1912
Lenin assumes management of the Bolshevik newspaper, *Pravda*. ***Titanic* sinks.*** First parachute jump from an airplane.

HEUER AND TAG HEUER

1907
Gemstone sales achieve record level of Swiss francs.

1908
Company obtains patent for **pulsometer**, still used in medicine today.

1910
Henri Freund & Bros. becomes Heuer's U.S. distributor. Products feature the brand name **The Rose** on dial or Rose Watch Co. on movement.

1911

Heuer introduces the **Time of Trip***, **first airplane and automobile dashboard chronograph**. Heuer obtains patent for calendar that charts length of pregnancy and expected delivery date. Jules-Edouard Heuer dies.

1912
Heuer launches production of bracelet wristwatches for women. Company is named **Ed. Heuer & Co. Rose Watch Company**. **Heuer logo** first appears on letterhead.*

1920 > 1923 > 1924 > 1927 > 1928 >

HISTORIC, CULTURAL, AND SCIENTIFIC EVENTS

1920
Women receive right to vote in the U.S. **Mahatma Gandhi begins nonviolent struggle for India's independence.** Piet Mondrian's first *Composition with Red, Yellow and Blue.**
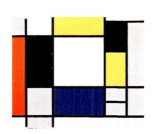

1923
Earthquake destroys Tokyo and Yokohama. Wireless telegraph between Italy and the U.S. First diesel-fueled truck manufactured. **First Le Mans auto races.***

1924
Stalin takes power in the U.S.S.R. upon Lenin's death. Hungarian Anatol M. Josepho invents the Photomaton. First Olympic Winter Games held in Chamonix. Barker and Skinner invent acrylic glass.

1927
Charles A. Lindbergh* makes first solo, nonstop flight across the Atlantic. Ford Model T is the world's leading car, with 15,070,033 produced.

1928
The first telephone connection between Europe and the U.S. Alexander Fleming discovers penicillin. Mickey Mouse first appears on screen. Bertolt Brecht and Kurt Weill compose *The Threepenny Opera*.

HEUER AND TAG HEUER

1920
The British army and postal service purchase **2,200 Heuer Time of Trip clocks**. Pocket chronographs, with split-seconds and chronometer certificates produced by Heuer, are chosen as **official timekeeping instruments for the Antwerp Olympic Games**. The brand, The Rose, is dropped. **Paul Vallette** models with LeCoultre movement are designed for the U.S. market.

1923

Hubert Heuer*, Charles-Auguste's second son, enters the company as the U.S. sales director. **Charles-Auguste Heuer dies.** The simple limited partnership Edouard Heuer & Co. is established on September 13, led by Charles-Edouard and Hubert Heuer.

1924
Heuer stops manufacturing pocket watches and focuses on wristwatches. Smith & Sons orders 1,200 Time of Trip clocks for airplanes. Pocket chronographs with split-seconds and chronometer certificates produced by Heuer, are chosen as the **official timekeeping instruments of the Paris Olympic Games.***

1927
Company's name changes to **Ed. Heuer, manufacturer of Jules Jürgensen watches**.

1928

Pocket chronographs with split-seconds and chronometer certificates produced by Heuer are chosen as **official timekeeping instruments of the Amsterdam Olympic Games.*** Heuer watches are put to the test as **Official Timekeeper** of ski, bobsleigh, and automobile races.

*pictured

> 1876   > 1878   > 1882   > 1883   > 1885

HISTORIC, CULTURAL, AND SCIENTIFIC EVENTS

Nikolaus Otto introduces his **first four-stroke fuel-powered engine**. Henry John Heinz invents tomato ketchup. Philadelphia World's Fair, organized on the 100th anniversary of American independence, marks beginning of the **"American watch crisis."**

University of London becomes first Bristish university to admit women.

Thomas Edison builds world's first electrical power plant in New York. Étienne-Jules Marey* invents chronophotographic gun, which records several phases of movements in one photo.

Universal Time system introduced. **Antonio Gaudí** begins work on La Sagrada Familia in Barcelona.* Orient Express line founded. **The Brooklyn Bridge, a suspension bridge,** is completed in New York.

Benz introduces the first **three-wheeled automobile with a gasoline engine**.

HEUER AND TAG HEUER

Edouard Heuer establishes London subsidiary, **E.D. Heuer, London**.

On September 1, Edouard Heuer establishes partnership with **Fritz Lambelet** and opens luxury watch and gemstone workshop. Edouard Heuer elected to the Bienne town council. **Louise Honorine***, Edouard Heuer's daughter, joins business as office apprentice and soon enters company management.

Edouard Heuer is one of the first watchmakers to **mass-produce pocket chronographs**.

Company earns silver medal at the **Amsterdam World's Fair** for its collection of pocket chronographs.

Heuer, Lambelet & Cie. dissolves. Company resumes using the name **Edouard Heuer & Cie**.

> 1892   > 1893   > 1895   > 1901   > 1902

HISTORIC, CULTURAL, AND SCIENTIFIC EVENTS

Loïe Fuller gives triumphant performance at the Folies Bergère in Paris.

Rudolf Diesel develops his engine. **Most Central European countries adopt Central European Time (CET).** First international photography exhibition held in Hamburg. Edvard Munch paints *The Scream.**

Wilhelm Röntgen discovers the X-ray. **Auguste and Louis Lumière produce their first films.**

The British engineer James Gibb obtains patent for the name "Ping Pong."* **Pablo Picasso holds first exhibit in Paris at Ambroise Vollard's gallery.** First Nobel Prizes awarded.

Auguste Verneuil announces discovery of the synthetic ruby. Bosch introduces high-tension magnetic ignition system for automobile motors. First auto race held in the Ardennes. Claude Debussy's premiere of *Pelléas and Mélisande* creates controversy.

HEUER AND TAG HEUER

Edouard Heuer dies on April 30 at the age of 52.

Charles-Auguste Heuer joins company management.

Heuer obtains patent for one of the **first water-resistant cases**. Heuer's catalogue already features **pocket watches* and brooch watches for women**.

La Chimère, Alligator, La Cigale, and Shamrock trademarks are registered.

Jules-Edouard and Charles-Auguste Heuer become exclusive owners of Edouard Heuer & Cie. Watch sales total 152,000 Swiss francs.

| 1860 > | 1864 > | 1867 > | 1869 > | 1870 > |

HISTORIC, CULTURAL, AND SCIENTIFIC EVENTS

1860 — **Abraham Lincoln elected president of the United States.** Southern states secede. Construction begins on London Underground.

1864 — Antonio Pacinotti invents a **dynamo that can be used as an electric motor.** The first short-duration chronometer, accurate to a quarter-second, appears.

1867 —  **United States buys Alaska from Russia** for $7.2 million. Canadian Confederation created. World's Fair* held in Paris. Félix Léon Edoux builds a hydraulic elevator. Typewriter patent filed in the United States.

1869 — Hydraulic energy used to produce electricity. **Suez Canal completed.** First transcontinental railway between New York and San Francisco established. **Switzerland adopts patent law.** Fridtjof Nansen crosses southern Greenland on skis.

1870 — New York Yacht Club's *Magic*, skippered by A. Comstock, wins the America's Cup.

HEUER AND TAG HEUER

1860 — **Edouard Heuer*, 20, opens watchmaking shop in Saint-Imier.** Marries Suzanna Scherz, daughter of a notary from Aeschi, in the Bernese Alps.

1864 — Edouard Heuer moves his business to Brügg and names it **Edouard Heuer & Cie.**

1867 — **Edouard Heuer establishes his business in the watchmaking region of Bienne.**

1869 —  Heuer obtains **patent for first independent crown-winding mechanism** for pocket watches.

1870 — Edouard Heuer buys house at 6 rue des Vergers in **Bienne.**

| 1887 > | 1888 > | 1889 > | 1890 > | 1891 > |

HISTORIC, CULTURAL, AND SCIENTIFIC EVENTS

1887 — Berliner introduces first gramophone. Augustus Desiré Waller performs first human electrocardiogram. American photographer Eadweard Muybridge publishes *Animal Locomotion.*

1888 — Heinrich Hertz proves existence of electromagnetic waves. Kodak* introduces first camera.

1889 —  First ascent of Africa's Mt. Kilimanjaro (5,895 meters). **The Eiffel Tower* is the symbol of the Paris World's Fair,** commemorating the 100th anniversary of the French Revolution. Six-day women's bicycle race held in New York.

1890 — John Boyd Dunlop produces his first tires. **Herman Hollerith* invents a tabulating machine that uses perforated cards, the first information-processing machine.**

1891 — Serious earthquake occurs in Japan. Otto Lilienthal makes **first glider flight.** First telephone line between Paris and London. The Trans-Siberian railway, 9,300 kilometers long, is built. **Construction begins on Chicago's first skyscraper, the Monadnock Building.**

HEUER AND TAG HEUER

1887 —  Heuer obtains French and German patents for famous **Oscillating Pinion.** Affected by the death of his daughter, Louise-Honorine, **Edouard Heuer turns over control to his son Jules-Edouard.***

1888 — Heuer obtains Swiss and English patents for **repeater watch with an automatic striking mechanism.**

1889 —  Heuer receives **silver medal** for its collection of pocket chronographs at the **Paris World's Fair.**

1890 — The **La Sirène** trademark is registered.

1891 —  After training in business, watchmaking, and gemology at the London firm of Edwin W. Streeter, **Edouard Heuer's third child, Charles-Auguste, becomes a Heuer employee.**

*pictured

LINK CALIBRE S CHRONOGRAPH

TAG HEUER FORMULA 1 GRANDE DATE CHRONOGRAPH

GRAND CARRERA CALIBRE 17 RS CHRONOGRAPH

THE 40TH ANNIVERSARY OF THE MONACO

Four decades after capturing the world's attention by appearing on the wrist of cinema legend Steve McQueen in the racing feature *Le Mans*, TAG Heuer's iconic Monaco chronograph was reissued in 2009 as a limited-edition timepiece. The perfect marriage of vintage sex appeal and modern cool, the 40th-anniversary chronograph features the same revolutionary elements as the classic 1969 Monaco, including the original Calibre 11 movement Dubois Dépraz. The first-ever self-winding automatic chronograph with microrotor, the Calibre 11 provides wearers with precision timing comparable to the standards of professional chronometer instruments. The latest iteration of the Monaco also pays homage to TAG Heuer's history by featuring the brand's original Heuer logo, which is flanked on the dial by two silver counters at 3 and 9 o'clock. The dark blue dial is further highlighted by fire-red minute, second, and hour hands, as well as luminescent markers and horizontal indexes. Stainless-steel push buttons at 2 and 4 o'clock, a date window at 6 o'clock, and curved, sapphire crystal with double anti-reflective treatment complete the watch's look.

The company chose Baselworld to present its Monaco *Twenty Four* Concept Chronograph. Based on the iconic exterior of Steve McQueen's square-shaped Monaco, the concept watch's unique tubular design and extreme shock-protected components are directly inspired by GT race-car technology.

TAG Heuer also launched the new Aquaracer 500M Calibre 5, the ultimate luxury watch inspired by the essence of water sports. Water-resistant to 500 meters, each model in this collection is equipped with the attributes of a high-performance diving watch, including a helium valve and a unidirectional turning bezel that ensures precise elapsed dive-time measurement. Highly luminescent markers on the hands and indexes, as well as an orange-tipped second hand, provide at-a-glance readability, either under water or in dim light. Additionally, the sapphire crystal and case back are scratch-resistant and anti-reflective for optimum visibility.

Together with Jack Heuer, and as a tribute to the pioneer of the automatic chronograph, TAG Heuer has decided to produce the Calibre 1887, a movement developed entirely in-house. At the same time, engineers in the TAG Heuer Quality Department are working on the Monaco V4.

The Calibre 1887 and the Monaco V4—along with the new Calibre Mikrograph 1/100th, an improvement of the Calibre 360 from 2005—will form a trilogy of exceptional movements that TAG Heuer will present in 2010, on the occasion of its 150th anniversary.

THE KNIGHTS OF TIME

Shot by renowned fashion photographer Tom Munro, the "What Are You Made Of?" campaign perfectly invokes TAG Heuer's spirit through a distinctive use of lighting and the resolute facial expressions of Leonardo DiCaprio, Tiger Woods, and Maria Sharapova in their respective ads. Each ambassador is photographed looking away from the camera with an introspective gaze, as if deep in thought about his or her next challenge. Instead of wearing a timepiece, the ambassadors hold it in their hands, emphasizing that a TAG Heuer is an extension of themselves and their personal journeys. Leonardo DiCaprio, the newest member of the TAG Heuer dream team, embodies this brand's notion of human achievement, he shares the same philosophy as TAG Heuer master watchmakers, who constantly question the process and strive to do better. To this end, Leonardo DiCaprio and TAG Heuer have forged a new partnership to support environmental charities. It is time to take responsibility for our future….

MONACO 40TH ANNIVERSARY RE-EDITION AUTOMATIC CHRONOGRAPH CALIBRE 11 LIMITED EDITION

CARRERA CALIBRE 16 DAY-DATE CHRONOGRAPH

AQUARACER 500M CALIBRE 5

It also dazzled the watchmaking world with the launch of the Link Calibre S, a new chronograph movement accurate to 1/100th of a second that combines the precision of quartz with the sophistication of mechanical functions.

The TAG Heuer 360 museum opened its doors in 2008 at the brand's headquarters in La Chaux-de-Fonds during a special ceremony attended by Formula One champion Lewis Hamilton. The world's first 360-degree watchmaking museum celebrates a century and a half of TAG Heuer history. Operated by a battery of 12 computers processing over one million images an hour, it is a unique and exhilarating showcase of the TAG Heuer story.

ETERNAL QUEST FOR EXCELLENCE

Introduced in 2007, the TAG Heuer Grand CARRERA is a premium collection of sophisticated timepieces, inspired by the spirit of modern GT cars and powered by the exclusive TAG Heuer Calibre RS, the first line of mechanical movements engineered with a rotating system. The indicators of this exclusive, GT engine-inspired rotating system enable watch-wearers to read small seconds and view a second time zone or chronograph time effortlessly, providing them with at-a-glance access to precision timing. At Baselworld 2008, the company presented the TAG Heuer Grand CARRERA Calibre 36 RS Caliper Concept Chronograph, the first automatic chronograph capable of measuring and displaying 1/10th of a second, thanks to its "Caliper" rotating scale. In 2008, it won the distinguished China's Most Successful Design Award, the Best Chronograph Prize at the Salón Internacional de Alta Relojería in Mexico, the Sports Watches Prize at the Grand Prix d'Horlogerie de Genève, and a Red Dot Design Award in 2009.

TAG Heuer was further encouraged in its quest for excellence when it became a privileged member of the Fondation de la Haute Horlogerie (FHH), the most exclusive club in the Swiss watchmaking industry.

TAG Heuer recorded another milestone with the launch of the MERIDIIST collection of mobile phones and accessories. As innovative in its design as its high-end technology, the world's first Swiss-made luxury communication instrument is the crowning achievement of 150 years of watchmaking know-how.

2008 was also an important year for TAG Heuer Avant-Garde Eyewear: The C-Flex concept received a SILMO Golden Award, the most prestigious prize in the eyewear industry. That year, TAG Heuer ambassador Vodafone McLaren Mercedes driver Lewis Hamilton won the highest honor in motor sport, clinching the FIA World Championship at the Brazilian Grand Prix to become Formula One's youngest world champion.

CHANGING THE FACE OF TIME

For TAG Heuer, prestige and performance are two constant factors that are also clearly apparent in terms of distribution strategy. Since the end of the '90s, the company has developed a network of highly selective boutiques, focusing on major cities.

In 2008, TAG Heuer decided to create a new boutique concept to bring its watchmaking culture to the whole world. The result: a timeless space which combines the past, present, and future. The first boutique was unveiled in Westfield, London, the largest shopping center in Europe. Then, after Singapore (Ion) and Tokyo (Ginza), the new concept traveled to several other cities around the world. To date, there are 73 TAG Heuer boutiques in 26 countries.

Alain Prost in his McLaren, 1986. Lewis Hamilton, 2008 Formula One World Champion; the TAG Heuer Monaco V4 Concept Watch, introduced in 2004; Maria Sharapova.

In 2002, the Micrograph F1, a descendant of the legendary Mikrograph of 1916, was awarded the Design Prize at the Grand Prix d'Horlogerie de Genève. It combined the aesthetics of a celebrated watch with the functions of a high-performance professional timekeeping instrument, and featured lap-measuring with a precision of 1/100th of a second, as well as a high-end digital screen for maximum readability. During this year, the company sponsored the BMW Oracle Racing team for the America's Cup with Chris Dickson and Peter Holmberg. To commemorate the partnership, TAG Heuer offered sea-racing fans a limited edition of the Link Searacer Oracle chronograph worn by all team members.

IN THE SPOTLIGHT

Just as the S/el—renamed Link—introduced a new era in watchmaking, a revolution was shaking up the otherwise peaceful world of golf. His name? Tiger Woods, arguably the greatest golfer in history. A worldwide TAG Heuer brand ambassador since 2003, Woods is unique, yet his motto speaks to us all: "The most important thing in life is to make yourself do better." TAG Heuer has followed this same philosophy for almost 150 years. The Link Calibre 36 chronometer, designed by Jack Heuer and endorsed by Tiger Woods, is a superlative example of the brand's relentless drive for perfection.

Launched in 2002, the advertising commercial "What Are You Made Of?" communicated the brand's daring personality and made a big impression internationally. In 2003, it starred Tiger Woods, shown hitting a golf ball that flies around the Monaco race circuit at the speed of a Formula One car. That same year, the long-awaited Sportvision line of optical and sun eyewear was launched, thrusting TAG Heuer's sporting prestige into an entirely new domain. The Physics range of the eyewear series received a prestigious Red Dot Design Award.

In 2003, TAG Heuer launched the Microtimer, fitted with the first Swiss electronic movement offering a remarkable precision of 1/1,000th of a second. A masterpiece of the miniaturization of complex electronics, the Microtimer is based on technology adapted from the demanding world of Formula One racing.

2004 ➤ 2010
AVANT-GARDE WATCHMAKING

In 2004, the company took on a new motor-racing challenge when it became the Official Timekeeper of the Indy Racing League (IRL) and the legendary Indy 500. No other racing circuit requires timing precision to 1/10,000th of a second. TAG Heuer took the watchmaking world by surprise when it launched a revolutionary concept watch at Baselworld 2004: the Monaco V4. Inspired by the brand's motor-racing heritage (the name comes from the engine-like V-formation of the movement's four barrels), this mechanical watch overturned basic watchmaking principles by featuring driving belts, linear mass, and ball bearings instead of conventional wheels and pinions. A totally new type of watch movement, it is considered the most astonishing advancement in mechanical watchmaking of the last decade, and it received a Red Dot Design Award in 2005.

FROM CONCEPT TO REALITY...

The Monaco *Sixty Nine*, another concept watch, went into full production in 2004, just a year after being unveiled at Baselworld. The first reversible watch with two different movements—one side features the Monaco dial with its mechanical hand-wound movement, the other the digital dial of the Microtimer with its 1/1,000th-of-a-second quartz chronograph movement—won the desirable Design Watches Prize at the Grand Prix d'Horlogerie de Genève.

At Baselworld 2005, TAG Heuer presented the most accurate mechanical timepiece ever crafted: the Calibre 360 Concept Chronograph. This timepiece is the first mechanical wrist chronograph to measure and display time to 1/100th of a second, thanks to the exceptionally high frequency of its balance wheel, which oscillates at 360,000 beats per hour, 10 times faster than any other chronograph. One year later, TAG Heuer picked up an esteemed Red Dot Design Award for this concept chronograph, and the movement has since been certified as a chronometer by C.O.S.C. (the Official Swiss Chronometer Control institute). Then, at Baselworld 2006, the most talked-about timepiece was the superlative Monaco Calibre 360 LS (Linear second) concept chronograph, a daring new timepiece with an all-new architecture that proudly displayed its unrivaled Calibre 360 LS precision technology. The TAG Heuer Carrera Calibre 360 Rose Gold Limited Edition, a prestige version of the Calibre 360 Concept Chronograph, was unveiled the same year and won the Sports Watches Prize at the Grand Prix d'Horlogerie de Genève.

TAG HEUER: THE SPORT AND GLAMOUR SUPERSTAR

In 2005, TAG Heuer gave depth and allure to its "Sports and Glamour" emphasis by signing new brand ambassadors: tennis superstar Maria Sharapova, Hollywood legends Uma Thurman and Brad Pitt, and racing aces Juan Pablo Montoya and Kimi Räikkönen.

The same year, Uma Thurman's favorite timepiece, the Haute Couture Diamond Fiction, was awarded the Ladies' Watches Prize at the Grand Prix d'Horlogerie de Genève. Fifty-four of its 879 diamonds display the time by channeling the light emitted by 54 LEDs.

In 2005, the first-ever Professional Golf Watch was launched, developed with the rigorous participation of Tiger Woods. It would go on to win a Chicago Athenaeum Good Design Award (2006) and a Fennia Prize (2007). TAG Heuer also named two new brand ambassadors from Formula One: Vodafone McLaren Mercedes drivers Fernando Alonso and Lewis Hamilton. They joined fellow competitor Kimi Räikkönen, the official driver for Scuderia Ferrari and 2007 FIA World Champion, who designed a new line of TAG Heuer Avant-Garde Eyewear.

SAILING TOWARD NEW ADVENTURES...

The TAG Heuer Aquaracer Calibre S revolutionized watchmaking with a groundbreaking innovation in chronograph movements: an in-house calibre which made it possible to measure and display watch, chronograph, and regatta functions with the same hands, thanks to its revolutionary "hybrid" construction comprising 230 electromechanical components. Patented for its synchronized bi-directional engines, reading format, and design concept, the chronograph won the prestigious *Popular Science* "Best of What's New" award in 2007.

ICONIC DESIGN

Baselworld 2007 was the stage for the 20th anniversary celebration of the TAG Heuer Link series. To commemorate the event TAG Heuer unveiled "SKIN," the most avant-garde booth ever built for the prestigious watch fair. This new booth won a Silver Award in *EXHIBITOR* Magazine's 23rd Annual Exhibit Design Awards competition in 2009!

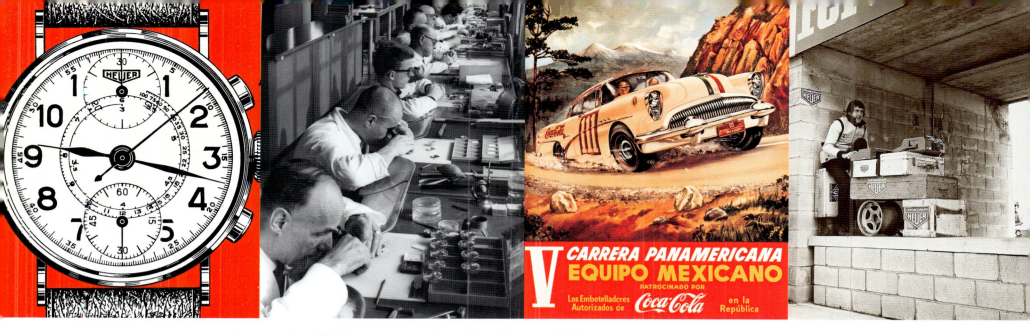

Heuer leaflet from 1945; Heuer workshop in Bienne, 18 rue Vérésius, April 1963; Carrera Panamericana, Equipo Mexicano poster; Jean Campiche and the Le Mans Centigraph during the 1,000-kilometer race at Nürburgring, 1973.

CARRERA

In 1963, Jack Heuer turned his creative focus to the world of cinema, designing the Film-Master, which measured film sequences in 16 mm and 35 mm. This made the brand a Hollywood and Bollywood favorite, with TAG Heuer timepieces worn in many movies and by today's stars, such as Leonardo DiCaprio and Shah Rukh Khan.

The following year, Jack Heuer turned to his overriding passion for motor racing with the inaugural launch of the legendary TAG Heuer Carrera. A tribute to professional motor racing's most grueling road race, the legendary Carrera Panamericana Mexico of the 1950s, this stunning piece of unconventional watchmaking technology was worn by numerous racing drivers. It remains one of TAG Heuer's most popular, timeless, and iconic creations.

In 1965, Jack Heuer unveiled a prototype of the Slalom Timer at the Basel Watch Fair. It was the company's first miniaturized electronic timing instrument accurate to 1/100th of a second. The electronic revolution had begun.

One year later, Jack Heuer stunned the watchmaking world again, this time by introducing the Microtimer, the world's first miniaturized electronic timing instrument accurate to an extraordinary 1/1,000th of a second.

The most famous sports event after the World Cup and the Olympic Games is the America's Cup. TAG Heuer was the Official Supplier of chronographs to the Intrepid team, which won the America's Cup in 1967.

MONACO: A SQUARE, WATER-RESISTANT CASE

In 1969, the Swiss driver Jo Siffert signed on as a TAG Heuer brand ambassador, becoming the first racing driver sponsored by a watch manufacturer.

At the beginning of the '60s, Jack Heuer reached an agreement with two other Swiss watch manufacturers to create the world's first automatic chronograph movement. They gave their top-secret project the confidential code name "99." The new Chronomatic Calibre 11 was launched in 1969. This first chronograph movement with an automatic microrotor mechanism powered both the TAG Heuer Carrera and Autavia, and also the legendary Monaco. This original automatic chronograph with a square, water-resistant case achieved a near-mythological status when Steve McQueen wore it in the film Le Mans (realesed 1971).

TIMING A LEGENDARY CAR

In 1971, Enzo Ferrari asked Clay Regazzoni, Swiss winner of the Italian Grand Prix, to find timing instruments for the 24 Heures du Mans race. TAG Heuer technology was ideally suited to the task, as demonstrated by the Le Mans Centigraph, which was able to measure time to 1/1,000th of a second. As Ferrari's Official Timekeeper from 1971 to 1979, the brand played a key role in the team's unprecedented string of world-championship victories, and saw its name linked to Ferrari legends such as Gilles Villeneuve, Niki Lauda, and Jody Scheckter.

Meanwhile, in Bienne, TAG Heuer continued to innovate. In 1973, the Microsplit 820 was unveiled, the first pocket quartz timing instrument precise to 1/100th of a second.

In 1975, TAG Heuer launched the Chronosplit, the world's first quartz wrist chronograph with a double digital display. The LCD on top showed the time of the day and the LED showed the stopped time to a precision of 1/10th of a second. Enzo Ferrari personally ordered 15 of these special Ferrari models. Other famous customers such as Paul Newman, soon joined the ranks of Chronosplit owners. Just two years later, the company presented the world's first digital-analog chronograph, the Chronosplit Manhattan GMT, forerunner of the Kirium Formula 1 chronograph.

1980 ➤ 2003
DESIGN INSPIRED BY TECHNOLOGY

The launch of the 2000 series in 1982 reinforced the unparalleled sporting spirit of the brand. This contemporary sports watch became an industry benchmark due to its six features: water-resistance up to 200 meters, a unidirectional turning bezel, uminescent hands and markers, a screw-in crown with a double gasket to ensure water resistance, a double safety clasp, and scratch-resistant, sapphire-crystal glass.

In 1984, Mike Birch broke the world record for the greatest distance sailed in 24 hours in his Formule Tag, the first Kevlar®-and-carbon-fiber catamaran. In 1985, TAG Heuer teamed up with McLaren Mercedes, forming what would become one of the longest-running and most successful partnerships in Formula One history; TAG Heuer was soon linked to some of the team's most famous drivers, including Alain Prost, Ayrton Senna, and Mika Häkkinen.

Launched in 1987, the S/el (sport and elegance) watch made its mark in the world of watchmaking, thanks to its signature feature: a double S-shaped bracelet. This famous watch reinforced TAG Heuer's position as the industry reference for sport, elegance, and prestige. The S/el was the favorite model of the legendary Ayrton Senna, who signed on as a TAG Heuer brand ambassador in 1988.

In 1989, TAG Heuer became the Official Timekeeper for World Cup alpine skiing events in the United States and Canada. In 1991, it also added the Indianapolis Motor Speedway, and in 1992, the Formula One World Championship. TAG Heuer used the most advanced technologiy to achieve a level of reliability comparable to that of atomic clocks. The timing of Formula One races, for example, was controlled by a GPS-satellite detection system, ensuring precision to a millionth of a second. In 1995, TAG Heuer was part of sailor Chris Dickson's challenge in the Louis Vuitton Cup, which reached the semifinals.

EMBLEMATIC CAMPAIGNS

In 1991, TAG Heuer launched the advertising campaign "Don't Crack Under Pressure," depicting the intense concentration exerted by athletes and emphasizing the mental, rather than physical, side of sport, pushing barriers to reach new heights of performance and greater standards of excellence. The next campaign, "Success. It's a mind game," began in 1995, and was not only striking but also entirely original. The advertisements depicted the mental pressure that athletes subject themselves to in order to win.

BRINGING THE PAST TO LIFE

TAG Heuer relaunched three of its classic series: TAG Heuer Carrera in 1996, Monaco in 1998, and Monza in 2001. In 1999, the company introduced the Link series, a bold reworking of the hugely successful S/el design. In 2003, it was the Autavia's turn once worn in the '60s by Swiss Formula One driver Jo Siffert. These watches were revised and modernized to offer functions that met contemporary needs, yet they remained faithful to the spirit of the original pieces and the brand's unique heritage.

In 2001, the Kirium Formula 1 represented the future direction of sports-watch design and a major technical achievement: a modern analog watch with digital chronograph functions and 1/100th-of-a-second precision. That same year, TAG Heuer became Official Timekeeper of the FIS Alpine Ski World Championships in St. Anton, Austria.

THE TAG HEUER STORY
TIMING THE WORLD'S PROGRESS SINCE 1860

1860 ➤ 1892
FROM ONE WORLD TO ANOTHER…

In 1860, at the age of 20, Edouard Heuer founded a watchmaking workshop in Saint-Imier, in the remote Jura mountains of Switzerland. It was the start of TAG Heuer's extraordinary story, which transformed the company originally named Heuer, after its founder, over 125 years into the company we know today.

THROWING AWAY THE KEY…

At this period in time, all watches were wound with a key. In 1869, two years after he moved his workshop to Bienne, Edouard Heuer changed the course of watchmaking history forever with his first patented invention: a keyless, crown-operated winding system. A huge success at the 1873 Universal Exhibition in Vienna, this new generation of timepieces soon became the most coveted in the world. When powerful American watch manufacturers moved aggressively into the European market, Edouard Heuer responded by pushing through innovations in every area of design, engineering, and manufacturing, thus helping to make Switzerland the world leader in the watchmaking industry.

…AND BANKING ON THE FUTURE

As sporting competitions rapidly expanded—on water, grass, cinder running tracks, and roads—measuring time accurately became increasingly important. Edouard Heuer acted upon this and, in 1882, he became one of the first to produce pocket chronographs in large quantities. In 1887, he patented one of the most important innovations in watchmaking: the famous Oscillating Pinion, still used to this day by leading manufacturers in the production of mechanical chronographs. Starting in 2010, this pinion will be used in the Calibre 1887, the fourth movement developed and produced in-house by TAG Heuer. The revolutionary device has allowed the chronograph to function very neatly by replacing the two large wheels of the anterior movements. With this breakthrough invention, TAG Heuer became the reference standard in chronographs and timing instruments for high-level sports. In 1889, at the Universal Exhibition in Paris, the company was awarded a silver medal for its pocket chronograph collection. When Edouard Heuer died in 1892, his creative vision and passion for innovation had laid the foundation for a watchmaking dynasty—one that was destined to make an indelible mark on the century that followed.

1893 ➤ 1949
TAG HEUER: MASTERING TIME

After Edouard Heuer's death, the company ownership passed to his two sons, Jules-Edouard and Charles-Auguste Heuer. Their daring and intuition brought TAG Heuer to the forefront of high-quality sports timing and chronographs.

INTERNATIONAL DEVELOPMENT

The two brothers were convinced that the company's future would unfold outside Switzerland. During a trip to London, Jules-Edouard and Charles-Auguste wrote to their mother: "It is useful to see, from time to time, how things are done elsewhere; you learn a great deal." They forged strong ties with local importers in other countries, such as Henry Freund in the United States. By this time, they had also seen an opportunity in sports, where there was an even greater demand for precision in timekeeping. The Time of Trip, patented in 1911, was the first 12-hour dashboard chronograph for cars and aircraft. It indicated the time and the duration of the journey. This innovation was a great success with aviation clubs. In 1919, the Zeppelin R34, with a Time of Trip on board, made the first flight over the North Atlantic. In 1929, Hugo Eckener equipped his Graf Zeppelin with this instrument before completing the first round-the-world trip in an airship.

CHASING 1/100th OF A SECOND

At the beginning of the 20th century, the timekeeping world was confronted with the challenge of increasing precision. Consequently, Charles-Auguste set a goal for his employees: "Make a stopwatch capable of a timekeeping precision five to ten times greater than anything that exists today." Thus, in 1916, the Mikrograph and Microsplit, and Semikrograph and Semicrosplit, were born. These were the world's first mechanical stopwatches that were accurate to 1/100th of a second and 1/50th of a second, respectively. At that time, other timing instruments could only measure to the nearest 1/5th of a second. This new development revolutionized science, industry, and watchmaking, and made TAG Heuer the natural choice as an official supplier of chronographs for the Olympic Games in Antwerp (1920), Paris (1924), and Amsterdam (1928). Thousands of Mikrographs were produced over the next six decades, until their discontinuation in 1969, thus providing TAG Heuer with a unique expertise in manufacturing movements that beat at 360,000 times an hour. The first alpine slalom and downhill ski races were timed by TAG Heuer, starting in 1928. Then, in the 1930s, the company proved itself, serving as the timekeeper of the speed-skiing race in St. Moritz and the Bobsleigh World Championship in Caux.

DEDICATED TO SCIENCE AND SPORT

In 1931, Professor Auguste Piccard, a specialist of cosmic radiation, led the first stratospheric flight. To commemorate the world-record altitude of 15,781 meters in a balloon, the city of Bienne gave Professor Piccard a gold TAG Heuer chronograph. In 1947, TAG Heuer presented him with another chronograph featuring hands with no radium, so it would not interfere with the cosmic-ray measurements. Hergé based the Professor Calculus character in the Tintin comic books on Professor Piccard.

In 1933, the company launched the Autavia (a combination of "AUTomobile" and "AVIAtion"), the first onboard stopwatch for cars and aircraft. This instrument was often mounted with a Hervue watch on a chrome base and affixed to a dashboard. TAG Heuer's cutting-edge chronographs soon appeared on the wrists of famous people around the world, including Harry S. Truman, Dwight D. Eisenhower, Henry Ford, Prince William of Sweden, and King Bhumibol of Thailand.

From the racetrack to the water, TAG Heuer continued to innovate. Since regatta timekeeping on Lake Geneva in the 1920s, sailing has inspired the company to use new materials and create new functions, as in 1950, when TAG Heuer unveiled its patented Mareograph, a unique sailing chronograph derived from the earlier Solunar watch, which let fishermen know when fish were feeding. Called the Seafarer in the United States, the new chronograph was the first with a tide indicator and a five-minute countdown function for sailing competitions.

1950 ➤ 1979
ACCELERATING RESEARCH AND INNOVATION

In 1955, TAG Heuer unveiled the Twin-Time, a GMT model that displayed two time zones simultaneously. In 1958, the company presented its famous onboard timer, the Rally-Master, consisting of a Master-Time (8-day clock) and a Monte-Carlo (12-hour stopwatch). The following year, Hubert Heuer and his nephew, Jack Heuer (son of Charles-Edouard), set up Heuer Time Corporation, a new American subsidiary based in New York.

On February 20, 1962, American astronaut John Glenn wore a TAG Heuer stopwatch when he piloted the Friendship 7 spacecraft on Mercury-Atlas 6, the first manned U.S. orbital mission, making TAG Heuer the first Swiss watchmaker in space!

the past to the stars of the future, our ambassadors read like a who's who of modern history: Edouard Heuer and Steve McQueen, Ayrton Senna and Leonardo DiCaprio, Lewis Hamilton and Shah Rukh Khan, Tiger Woods and Maria Sharapova. Together they all share a strong determination to achieve their ultimate goals, pushing the limits of what is possible through hard work and mental strength. We cannot know what the future holds, but we do know that if we continue to look forward, we will be the ones who shape it.

Jean-Christophe Babin

First workshop owned by Edouard Heuer in Bienne, Switzerland.

From a small workshop in the Swiss Jura mountains, TAG Heuer has transformed into a watchmaking legend. Recognized throughout the world for its luxury sports watches and pioneering work in chronographs, TAG Heuer watches epitomize prestige and performance, brilliantly fusing technology with design. TAG Heuer has revolutionized 150 years of watchmaking history through a constant pursuit of excellence and innovation, maintaining a strong link between the company of today and the people who have shaped its history. From heroes of

PIONEERING SWISS WATCHMAKING FOR 150 YEARS

TAGHEUER150YEARS

SWISS AVANT-GARDE SINCE 1860

ASSOULINE